GALLIPOLI 1915

GENERAL EDITOR DAVID G. CHANDLER

OSPREY
MILITARY

CAMPAIGN SERIES

OSPREY
MILITARY

GALLIPOLI 1915

FRONTAL ASSAULT ON TURKEY

PHILIP J. HAYTHORNTHWAITE

◄ *A captured Turkish trench on Bolton's Ridge, Anzac, on 26 April. Private J. B. Bryant (8th Victoria Battalion) holds an old shell-case at the entrance to a dugout. (Australian War Memorial, neg. no. A 3869)*

First published in 1991 by
Osprey Publishing, Elms Court, Chapel
Way, Botley, Oxford OX2 9LP,
United Kingdom.
Email: info@ospreypublishing.com

Also published as Campaign 8
Gallipoli 1915

ISBN 1 84176 030 7

Cover image courtesy of the
Australian War Memorial, neg. no.
G 599.

Produced by DAG Publications Ltd
for Osprey Publishing Ltd. Colour
bird's eye view illustration by Cilla
Eurich. Cartography by Micromap.
Wargaming Gallipoli by Bob Cordery.
Wargames consultant Duncan
Macfarlane. Typeset by Ronset
Typesetters Ltd, Darwen,
Lancashire. Mono camerawork by
M&E Reproductions, North
Fambridge, Essex.
Printed in China
through World Print Ltd.

Acknowledgement
The author wishes to express his
grateful thanks to the Australian War
Memorial, Canberra, for their
assistance in providing some of the
illustrations reproduced here.

▶ *Top: ANZACs in a
Turkish trench at Lone
Pine, showing how some
Turkish positions were
roofed-over with logs to
turn them into most
formidable strongpoints.
Note the different ways of
wearing the Australian
slouch hat! (Australian
War Memorial, neg. no.
A 2022)*

CONTENTS

FOR A CATALOGUE OF ALL BOOKS PUBLISHED BY OSPREY
MILITARY, AUTOMOTIVE AND AVIATION PLEASE WRITE TO:

The Marketing Manager, Osprey Direct USA, PO Box 130,
Sterling Heights, MI 48311-0130, USA. Email: info@OspreyDirectUSA.com

The Marketing Manager, Osprey Direct UK, PO Box 140, Wellingborough,
Northants, NN8 4ZA, United Kingdom. Email: info@OspreyDirect.co.uk

VISIT OSPREY'S WEBSITE AT:

http://www.ospreypublishing.com

◀ *Troops crowd the beach at Anzac Cove, a scene repeated throughout the campaign as supplies were moved in and casualties evacuated; such movements continued even during the final withdrawal, so as not to alert the Turks to the imminence of the ANZAC departure. A medical unit is shown in the foreground: note the red cross brassards and folded stretcher. (Australian War Memorial, neg. no. PS 1659)*

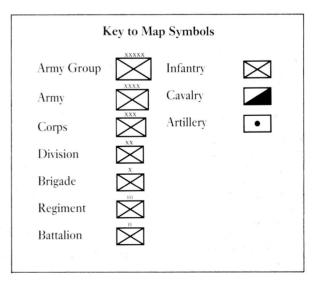

Key to Map Symbols

Army Group	XXXXX	Infantry	
Army	XXXX	Cavalry	
Corps	XXX	Artillery	
Division	XX		
Brigade	X		
Regiment	III		
Battalion	II		

ORIGINS OF THE CAMPAIGN

The expedition to the Dardanelles was a direct result of the deadlock which arose on the Western Front with the beginning of trench warfare after the first weeks of the First World War; but its origins lay in the confused sphere of Balkan politics.

Long regarded as 'the sick man of Europe', the tottering Ottoman Empire had suffered the repressive rule of Sultan Abdul Hamid II ('the Damned') from August 1876 until his deposition in 1909. The new Sultan then installed was Mohammed V, Abdul the Damned's younger brother, but he was merely a figurehead: all power was concentrated in the hands of the instigators of Abdul's overthrow, the 'Young Turks'. This youthful group of politicians, revolutionaries and opportunists restored the constitution abolished by Abdul in 1877, but ran the empire with equal tyranny. They were an odd collection: Talaat Bey, the political leader, who was the real controller of the empire; Djavid Bey, Finance Minister, a Jewish financier from Salonika; and, most significantly, Enver Pasha, the half-Albanian War Minister who had fought against the Italians in Libya and in the Balkan War of 1912-13, during which he had shot the then War Minister for endeavouring to arrange a peace which he saw as disadvantageous to Turkey. Enver was hated by the empire's minority groups, by the older generation of the politicians who had supported Abdul the Damned, and by the army, following his dismissal of 1,200 politically suspect officers in 1913; but he remained the power behind the Young Turk government.

By 1914 Turkey's financial situation was critical, desperately weakened by the Balkan Wars. Within the government were conflicting views on foreign aid: Minister of Marine Djemal, for example, favoured a French alliance, but the dominant voice was Enver's, whose experience as military attaché in Berlin had convinced him of the advantages of closer ties with Germany. These were cemented by early 1914 with the arrival of the German Military Mission, requested by the Young Turks and given the task of reorganizing the Turkish army. Led by General Liman von Sanders, it had begun its work with considerable effect.

In the event of a European war, Turkey's geographical position was crucial. Half Russia's exports (nine-tenths of her grain) passed through the Bosphorus and the Dardanelles, this route being Russia's main contact with her allies, Britain and France. It was thus of great importance to those nations that Turkey remain neutral in the event of hostilities, but two days before the outbreak of war, Germany and Turkey agreed an alliance against Russia, but one which did not commit Turkey to military action. Great indignation was aroused in Turkey when, on the following day, two dreadnought battleships which had been built in Britain for the Turkish navy, and which were almost completed, were requisitioned by Britain (*Sultan Osman I*, which became HMS *Agincourt*, and *Reshadieh*, which became HMS *Erin*). This played into German hands: immediately, as a gesture of solidarity, they sent the battlecruiser *Goeben* and the light cruiser *Breslau* to Turkey, to become part of the Turkish Navy. Enver, temporarily seeming to have lost his nerve and currently negotiating a Russo-Turkish alliance, was informed when the two ships had evaded the British fleet in the Mediterranean and were waiting to enter the Dardanelles; to admit them would be to confirm Turkey's links with Germany to the exclusion of the Allies. He ordered them to sail through.

The Allies became increasingly alarmed at the possibility of Turkish entry into the war, and by early September the British Naval Mission (which

The European Situation, January 1915

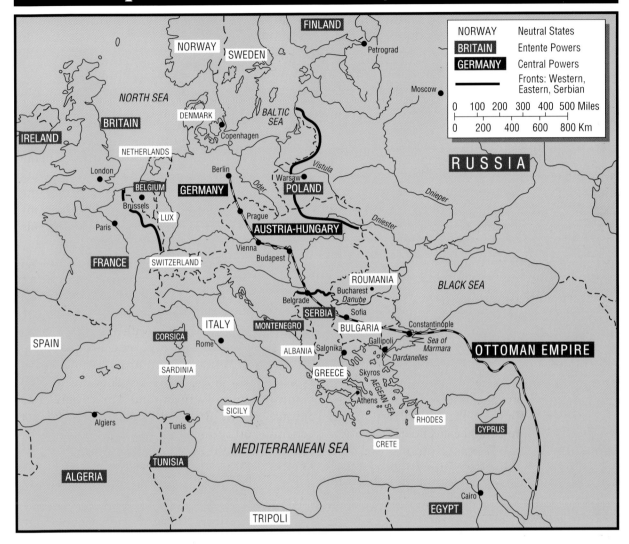

had been training the Turkish Navy) was with-drawn; German command was consequently ex-tended to the Turkish Navy. Without orders from the Turkish government, the German commander of the Dardanelles fortifications (Weber Pasha) closed the waterway, in direct contravention of international law; but Enver and Talaat had so delivered Turkey into German control that despite protestations from some members of the govern-ment, Turkey was now firmly in the German camp. On 29/30 October *Goeben*, *Breslau* and other vessels, nominally Turkish but crewed partly by Germans, bombarded Russian shore establish-ments on the Black Sea coast; Djemal claimed

ignorance of the raid, but probably Enver and Talaat had been informed. Russia, Britain and France issued an ultimatum to the Turkish government, and when it remained unanswered hostilities began officially on 31 October 1914.

By the beginning of 1915 it was obvious that the war would be protracted; trench-lines ran from the North Sea to Switzerland, and already it was obvious that on this 'Western Front' a rapid decisive victory was unlikely. Russia, in addition to fighting the Turks in the Caucasus, had suffered severely on the Eastern Front, at the battles of Tannenberg and the Masurian Lakes, and it was feared that their military effort might collapse if

the Germans launched an offensive of major significance. In an attempt to relieve the pressure on Russia came the plan to attack the Dardanelles.

The genesis of the idea originated before the outbreak of war, in discussions between the Secretary of State for War, Lord Kitchener, and Winston Churchill, First Lord of the Admiralty, although their original plan was for the expedition to be undertaken by Greece, at that time in sympathy with the Allied powers. King Constantine of Greece, however, was related by marriage to the German Kaiser Wilhelm II, and had become increasingly pro-German.

Upon the receipt of a plea from Russia for help in distracting Turkish resources, the Dardanelles plan was resurrected and discussed in the British War Council. Initially Churchill and Lord Fisher (First Sea Lord) considered a Greek landing on the Gallipoli peninsula, which took its name from the main town and was the key to the Dardanelles and the passage to the Sea of Marmara, to Constantinople and thence to the Black Sea. This would be accompanied by a Franco-British

▲*The German-Turkish alliance: the visit of Kaiser Wilhelm II to the Sultan. To the Kaiser's left are Enver Pasha, Talaat Bey (background, dark uniform), Abbas Hilme the ex-Khedive, and Rifaat Bey, chairman of the Turkish senate. (Australian War Memorial, neg. no. H 12323)*

landing on the Asiatic side of the channel, with the Dardanelles being forced by a squadron of old British battleships which, being outdated, could not be risked in a battle with the German fleet and were thus regarded as expendable. Churchill was interested especially in this latter concept, despite the difficulties that had been experienced when Admiral Duckworth's British fleet had attempted the same manoeuvre, unsuccessfully, in 1807. The concept, however, was sound; once the fleet had overcome the decrepit Turkish shore-batteries and entered the Sea of Marmara, it was hoped that Greece (if not already in the Allied camp), Bulgaria, and perhaps Roumania and Italy, would abandon their neutrality and join a Balkan coalition against Turkey; and securing the Dardanelles

▲ Field Marshal Colmar von der Goltz, 1843–1916, the first German organizer of the Turkish Army (1883–95), and from November 1914 attached to Turkish headquarters as adviser to the Sultan. He later commanded in Mesopotamia but died in 1916, having been poisoned, it is thought, by the 'Young Turks'.

▲ Defences of the Dardanelles: a German cartoon showing the entrance to the Dardanelles guarded by rocks in the shape of von der Goltz (left) and Liman von Sanders.

and Sea of Marmara would allow Russian ships again to pass from the Black Sea to the Mediterranean, enabling munitions to be delivered to Russia and Russian grain to the western Allies. The plan, which has been termed the only truly innovative strategic concept of the entire war, met with approval from both politicians and military authorities; Kitchener's approval was doubtless greatly influenced by the fact that few military resources were envisaged, and thus the effort on the Western Front would not be compromised. It was believed that the appearance of a British fleet off Constantinople might cause the downfall of the Turkish government, and as Turkey's only two munitions factories were within range of naval gunfire, even a short bombardment (against which the Turks were believed to be powerless to reply) could effectively remove Turkey from the war at a stroke. Russia received the plan with enthusiasm, and France offered a naval squadron to serve under British command in the great enterprise against Constantinople.

As the plan progressed, an increasing number of British ships was allocated for the expedition, even the new HMS *Queen Elizabeth*, one of the most powerful ships afloat; but at this stage Admiral Lord Fisher voiced deep misgivings. His relations with Churchill, 34 years his junior, were extremely cordial; until at the height of the planning Fisher turned against the whole scheme, perhaps feeling that Churchill was over-stretching the navy or fearing that the Dardanelles would appropriate resources needed to combat the German fleet in the North Sea. He expressed his fears in logical argument (notably that even if the old battleships were expendable, their experienced crews were not), but having threatened to resign eventually decided to support the expedition.

On 1 March 1915 the Greek government of the pro-Allied Eleutherios Venizelos offered three divisions for a landing on the Gallipoli peninsula and an eventual advance on Constantinople. Such a plan was accepted by Britain and France, but Russia hesitated from a fear of the expansion of Greek power; when this view became known in Greece the Venizelos government fell and was replaced by a pro-German ministry. The provision of a military contingent therefore fell upon Britain and France. Encouraged by Fisher, Kitchener eventually inclined towards a British landing, and despite protests from those wishing to concentrate the available resources on the Western Front, agreed to allocate the British 29th Division, and the Australian and New Zealand divisions recently arrived in Egypt, to support the naval operations. To command this military wing, Kitchener selected his old colleague Ian Hamilton.

With the dispatch of the military contingent, the Mediterranean Expeditionary Force (the original appellation, 'Constantinople Expeditionary Force', had been changed upon Hamilton's insistence that it made the destination too obvious to the Turks), the events were set in motion for the most severe British military reverse of the entire war. Great criticism has been levelled against all involved, much of it entirely justified; but the appalling mismanagement which occurred should not obscure the essential feasibility of the concept. Had the venture succeeded, its effect on the course of the war could have been immense, perhaps even forestalling the collapse of Imperial Russia; but the execution of the plan was beset by ineptitude, from which hardly any politician or senior military leader emerges with credit. The gallantry of the troops became a legend which compared favourably with the Trojan Wars, the site of which was so near to the Gallipoli battle-front that countless writers remarked upon the comparison between Hamilton's expedition and that of Agamemnon and Menelaus ('Stand in the trench, Achilles,/Flame-capped, and shout for me', as wrote Patrick Shaw-Stewart of the Royal Naval Division; he survived Gallipoli but was killed in 1917). Yet the greatest tragedy of the campaign was that the conduct of the expedition was unworthy of the courage of the troops who were sacrificed upon its altar.

◀ Ian Hamilton and his staff, including French officers; Hamilton is at centre left, immediately to the right of the Scottish officer wearing the glengarry.

THE COMMANDERS

It could be argued that the most influential figures in the Gallipoli campaign were those who never (or only briefly) set foot upon the peninsula; and it should be remembered that the nominal commanders-in-chief did not enjoy total freedom of action, but were constrained by their respective governments.

The Allied Commanders

Perhaps the most central figure in the campaign was the Allied commander, Sir Ian Standish Monteith Hamilton. A Scot born in Corfu, Hamilton was aged 62 in 1915 and had spent his entire adult life in the army, had seen more active service than almost any other general officer and was apparently totally without fear, as witnesses of his conduct in action testify. His staff experience was wide; ADC to Roberts in India, Military Secretary to Sir George White and deputy to Kitchener in the last stages of the Boer War, followed by important posts at the War Office and a visit to the Russo-Japanese War. He was highly intelligent, with great talents for writing and poetry; Hamilton was essentially a sensitive man who was too considerate and too good-natured for the task he had been given. He stood very much in Kitchener's shadow and was loath to question the directives of his chief, and thus was denied the opportunity of imposing his will upon the course of the campaign, but even if he had been given greater freedom of action, it is doubtful whether he would have exploited it. A degree of ruthlessness was required to order his subordinates to act, to dismiss those who were patently inept, yet such was Hamilton's nature that he only advised, and having given a broad outline of his strategy left the implementation of it entirely to his generals. He urged instead of ordered and believed that a suggestion of an obvious course of action was sufficient, not

▲ *Sir Ian Standish Monteith Hamilton (1853–1947), commander of the Mediterranean Expeditionary Force.*

realizing that his subordinates lacked drive or the intelligence he possessed. Even when this became obvious, he was unwilling to impose his own command; alone of the generals he appreciated the significance of the unopposed landing at 'Y' Beach, and was in a position to order an immediate reinforcement and advance which might well have achieved the objective of the landing at a stroke; yet he declined to act. He remained far from the scene of the action, aboard ship and later on Imbros, and this divorce from the realities of the campaign perhaps contributed to the over-optimistic tone of his reports. Brave, charming and

◀ Kitchener (left) and Birdwood at Anzac, during the visit that convinced Kitchener that further efforts at Gallipoli were hopeless.

▶ Lieutenant-General Sir William Birdwood, later Lord Birdwood of Anzac and Totnes, commander of the Australian and New Zealand Army Corps and described by Hamilton as 'the soul of Anzac'.

▶ Far right: Sir Aylmer Hunter-Weston (front), commander of the 29th Division and later VIII Corps, with two staff officers (identified by their red gorget-patches) at the entrance to the general's dugout.

almost universally liked, Hamilton was essentially a weak commander given a task beyond his abilities and resources.

If Hamilton bears some of the blame for the mismanagement of the campaign, much of it must be accorded to Field Marshal Lord Kitchener of Khartoum, Secretary of State for War. Sixty-five years old in 1915, 'K of K' was the great hero of the British public after successful colonial exploits; but he was never liked by his political associates and behaved in an offhand, authoritarian manner. His actions over the Dardanelles campaign were ill-conceived, he delayed sending the military forces, then sent them terribly unprepared, kept them short of supplies and reinforcement, and appointed the wrong generals. His authority had been unchallenged, but his death when HMS *Hampshire* was torpedoed in 1916 probably saved him from eclipse; the universal public lamentation of his loss was not felt to the same degree by his associates in the government.

Lieutenant-General Sir William Birdwood, the 50-year-old commander of the Australian and New Zealand Army Corps, and described by Hamilton as 'the soul of Anzac', was one of the best Allied commanders. A 'Kitchener man' who had served as 'K''s military secretary in India, he established a great rapport with the Australasian troops, who took 'Birdie' to their hearts, and his handling of the latter stage of the campaign suggests that he would have been a better choice for supreme command. It is much to be regretted that Birdwood's four-point order issued to the ANZACs in April was not appreciated by other commanders in the campaign; 'Concealment wherever possible; covering fire always; control of fire and control of your men; communications never to be neglected.' His admiration for the ANZAC troops was unbounded and when raised to the peerage he took as his title 'of Anzac and Totnes'.

Lieutenant-General Sir Aylmer Hunter-Weston, first commander of VIII Corps, though personally a charming man, was devoid of imagination and apparently unable to learn from his mistakes; his throwing of men into attack after hopeless attack slaughtered his command and demonstrated an alarming inability to appreciate what was feasible. Lieutenant-General the Hon. Sir Frederick Stopford, commander of IX Corps,

was another of Kitchener's disastrous appointments. Aged 61, Stopford was selected simply on grounds of seniority, having seen only limited service (Buller's military secretary in the Boer War) and having never commanded in battle. A kindly man but patently completely inept, he was allowed to remain in command at Suvla by Hamilton's customary courtesy, and it was probably to Stopford's relief that he was finally relieved of his duty, but far too late. He might have been less of a liability with a perceptive chief of staff, but his was Brigadier-General Hamilton Reed, who had won a VC at Colenso in circumstances of great gallantry, but whose tactical thinking was dominated totally by an insistence on heavy bombardment, and thus Stopford's unwillingness to execute the rapid advances needed immediately after the Suvla landing was compounded by the opinions of his chief of staff.

Rear-Admiral Sackville Carden was not as resolute in his attitudes to a naval attack as his original planning might have implied, and the responsibility appears to have affected his health

▶ *Rear-Admiral Sackville Carden.*

seriously. He had been appointed to command from his position as superintendent of the dock-yard at Malta only because the real Dardanelles expert, Admiral Limpus, had been head of the naval mission in Turkey and whose appointment to the fleet (at a time when Turkey was still neutral) would have given offence to that nation. Carden's successor, Vice-Admiral Sir John de Robeck, was an experienced officer used to the Mediterranean, but his concern over his losses and his belief that an unaided naval operation was futile helped to precipitate the military forces into their terrible situation. Sharply contrasting was the attitude of his deputy, Commodore Roger Keyes, a young and energetic officer so committed to Churchill's original concept that even at the last was still agitating for a renewed naval assault, when the real chance of success had long gone. Keyes' enthusiasm gained him supporters, but his comparatively lowly rank frustrated his attempts to salvage the situation.

Of the generals in subsidiary command, a few exhibited the frightening incapacity of their seniors: Sir Alexander Godley, commanding the New Zealand and Australian Division at Anzac, was in the Hunter-Weston mould of 'success at any price', and Brigadier-General F.E. Johnston, who commanded one of the columns in the attack on Sari Bair, was irresolute and unfitted to command. Others were conspicuously successful, notably Sir William T. Bridges (mortally wounded at Anzac), Major-General Herbert V. Cox of 29 Indian Brigade, and the Australian brigade-commanders John Monash and Harry Chauvel, both of whom won considerable fame later in the war. The late replacements, Generals Byng, Maude and Maxwell, were all capable comman-ders, but they replaced the incompetents too late for their presence to make much impact.

The original French commander was General Albert d'Amade, 59 years old and experienced in North African warfare. His early service on the Western Front ended with the precipitate retreat of his forces and he was dismissed from command. A charming and popular man, his lack of convic-tion and pessimism were manifested again at

Helles, compounded by strain, responsibility and the recent loss of a son, and Hamilton welcomed his replacement. This was Henri Gouraud, aged 48 and known as 'the Lion of the Argonne' from recent service, who was popular with his men and fearlessly brave. He regarded the Dardanelles expedition as the only true manoeuvre to be attempted since the outbreak of war and was of the opinion that similar manoeuvres, for example a landing at Bulair, were the key to success. Contrasting with Hamilton's isolation from his troops, Gouraud's regular tours of the trenches were instrumental in maintaining morale, but his injury on 30 June was an irreparable loss. Hamilton, who viewed Gouraud as one of the finest generals he had ever met, felt the loss most keenly, especially as his replacement was the divisional commander Maurice Bailloud, recalled from retirement at the age of 67 and described as a stupid pessimist. The French naval commander, Rear-Admiral Emile Guépratte, was a Gallic version of Keyes in that he was anxious to press on with the naval attack at all costs. Fearless and able to act on his own initiative,

▲ *Sir William Bridges, first Chief of the Australian General Staff and commander of the Australian Imperial Force; he was mortally wounded by a sniper on 15 May.*

◄ *Vice-Admiral Sir John de Robeck (front row, centre) and his staff; the officer seated to de Robeck's right is Commodore Roger Keyes.*

▶ En route *to the Dardanelles, General Albert d'Amade presents Colours to a French battalion.*

◄General Henri Gouraud (third from left) and his staff at Helles.

◄Below left: Commander of the French contingent after Gouraud was wounded: General Maurice Bailloud.

►Otto Liman von Sanders, (1855–1929) wearing Turkish uniform. He was head of the German Military Mission to Turkey and defender of Gallipoli.

►Far right: Mustafa Kemal, heart of the Turkish defence, photographed at Gallipoli, (Australian War Memorial, neg. no. A 5319)

his collaboration with the British (under whose command he placed his ships without hesitation) was entirely cordial and greatly appreciated by all those with whom he came into contact, save his own superiors: in May 1915, without explanation, the French Vice-Admiral Nicol was installed over his head as being a commander less likely to hazard everything in support of the British. Guépratte's continued advocacy of a naval assault finally led to his removal to shore duty in October 1915.

The Turkish Commanders

The Turkish command was very much dominated by Liman von Sanders and Mustafa Kemal. Otto Liman von Sanders was a cavalry officer aged sixty in 1915. The head of Germany's military mission to Turkey, he became Inspector of the Turkish Army and was given command of the Turkish forces in the Caucasus upon the outbreak of war, but in March 1915 was transferred to command the Fifth Army on the Gallipoli peninsula. His introduction of German officers into positions of responsibility was greatly beneficial, though the

language difficulties caused some confusion, few Germans being able to speak Turkish. His arrangements for the defence of the Dardanelles were well-conceived, and his conduct during the campaign was markedly different from that of Hamilton. Though his actions were hardly inspired (he miscalculated the main threat at the first landing), he never hesitated to amend his plans, and was more decisive and more in touch with the front line. His relationship with his subordinates was also decisive; he had no hesitation in dismissing Feizi Bey at the start of the Suvla operation, and gave Mustafa Kemal the responsibility which his talents justified, despite his comparatively junior rank. Liman von Sanders' relations with his superiors were never easy; Enver Pasha was antagonistic from the outset, and in late July his masters in Germany were sufficiently concerned that they requested he return home for consultation, which was forestalled by the Suvla landing.

Enver Pasha, despite his high position, had a poor grasp of military affairs. Aged only 34 in 1915, he had seen some active service in the Italo-Turkish War, but the operations he conducted were marked by a conspicuous lack of success. His planning was faulty (his original dispositions for the defence of the Dardanelles were bad), and his relations with Limon von Sanders were very poor. Although he had little to do with the defence of the Gallipoli peninsula (save interfere), he took the credit for it. Enver's relations with his subordinates seem to typify the jealousy and lack of co-operation which afflicted the entire Turkish command.

A very different proposition was Mustafa Kemal. Aged 34 in 1915, his career had fluctuated between banishment for sedition (1904) to service in the Italo-Turkish and Balkan Wars. Lacking a capability for negotiation or compromise and dismissive of opinions that conflicted with his own, Kemal's abilities were submerged by Enver's rise, and conflict between the two was inevitable. But whereas Enver was militarily inept, Kemal had a superb grasp of strategy and an ability to inspire his troops by his reckless bravery in action. Liman von Sanders respected his abilities, but he was a difficult subordinate and this, combined with the conflict with Enver, prevented his immediate promotion. Kemal's energetic handling of his troops throughout the Gallipoli campaign not only

put heart into the Turkish defence, but on a number of occasions proved decisive in thwarting the Allied plans.

Essad Pasha, nominally Kemal's superior, played a much less important role. Upon the landing at Anzac, it was Kemal who grasped that Chunuk Bair and the Sari Bair ridge were the key to the whole situation, and his actions in committing more troops than ordered were quite beyond his authority; in presenting Essad with a *fait accompli*, Kemal virtually took the command into his own hands despite his lowly rank as a divisional commander. It was fortunate for the Turks that he did; Essad's inability to appreciate the threat posed by the Suvla position (which was obvious to Kemal, though his opinions were ignored by Essad) suggests that without Kemal, a very different outcome might have transpired.

◀ *A typical Turkish infantryman wearing the greenish-khaki field uniform adopted from 1909, basically of German style, with brown leather equipment, khaki puttees (officers generally wore knee-boots), and the enverieh or 'Enver Pasha helmet', originally a turban but later made of cloth wrapped around a straw framework, producing a distinctive sun-helmet. Such 'regulation' appearance was far from universal: shortages of equipment were endemic in the Turkish Army, so that many lacked items of uniform and some were clothed virtually in rags. The rifle is the Turkish version of the German Mauser. (Painting by Cilla Eurich)*

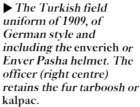

▶ *The Turkish field uniform of 1909, of German style and including the* enverieh *or Enver Pasha helmet. The officer (right centre) retains the fur tarboosh or kalpac.*

THE OPPOSING ARMIES

The Turkish Army

Despite the efforts of the German Military Mission and the employment of experienced German commanders, the Turkish Army at the outbreak of war was a very imperfect body, which led to its being seriously under-rated by the Allied commanders and politicians.

The Ottoman Army was recruited by conscription, for which all those of 18 years and over were liable. According to the Army Act of 12 May 1914 the enlistment period was 25 years for the infantry, 20 for other arms and 17 for the navy, of which active service in the *Nizam* or regular forces was 2, 3 and 5 years respectively. (Members of the Sultan's family were not liable for service; students served a shorter term, the physically unfit paid a tax instead, and exemption from serving more than five months could be purchased. Christians and Jews were restricted to labour battalions.) After this period of *Nizam* service, the men joined the

▲ *The Turkish army was habitually short of uniform and equipment: this typical soldier wears a cloth skull-cap instead of the* enverieh *and simple 'native' sandals instead of boots.*

reserve (*Redif*) of which, from 1898, there were two classes, *Redif* Class I and the *Ilaweh*, styled *Redif* Class II from 1903. Both existed only as cadres in peacetime, with the intention that in time of war *Redif* Class I would be mobilized rapidly, and Class II ultimately being absorbed into Class I. For those men reaching the end of their period of service there existed the *Mustahfiz*, a territorial militia which did not maintain even a cadre in peacetime.

The Turkish forces were initially divided into three armies, increased to four in September 1914 (with headquarters at Constantinople, Baghdad, Damascus and Erzinjan), and ultimately to nine. The number of corps allocated to each army varied with circumstances, with two or three divisions comprising a corps. In August 1914 36 divisions existed (ultimately 34 more were more mobilized), but many were very under-strength. In peacetime a *Nizam* division supposedly consisted of 13 infantry battalions, a cavalry squadron, 24 guns and supporting services, with a total strength of about 15,500 men, increasing to about 19,000 in wartime. To each *Nizam* division would be added a *Redif* division to form an Army Corps. From the beginning, however, Turkish formations only rarely reached their establishment; those divisions which in peacetime were kept at half-strength were often only at quarter-strength, and even after wartime mobilization many divisions only reached about one-third of their establishment. The actual field strength of a division comprised three regiments of three battalions each, each battalion of four companies; battalion-strength was supposedly about 700 men and 24 officers for *Nizam* battalions, 900 men and 24 officers for *Redif* I and 800 men and 24 officers for *Redif* II.

Artillery, traditionally an independent command, was similarly under-strength, but all were *Nizam* troops and none reservists; it was divided into field, fortress and depot branches, the former including also the horse, mountain and howitzer regiments. Each division supposedly included a field regiment of two or three battalions, each of three 4-gun batteries; each three-division corps had two mountain batteries and a howitzer battalion (6-gun batteries); each cavalry brigade included two horse artillery batteries, one cavalry brigade normally serving with each corps. Each division thus maintained, on paper, between 24 and 36 field-guns. The artillery was equipped with the 75mm Krupp field-gun, and the 1905-pattern 75mm Krupp and 75mm Schneider mountain guns, but older, 87mm German field-guns and antiquated smooth-bored howitzers were also in service. Only a few modern heavy guns were available (150mm Krupp and Schneider-Creusot howitzers), and fortress artillery was even more obsolete.

The equipment of the Turkish Army was similarly supposed to have been of 'modern' design, a German-style greenish-khaki uniform having been introduced from 1909, with 'arm-of-service' colours worn on the collar (infantry khaki, light infantry olive-green, artillery dark blue, cavalry light grey, engineers light blue, train red, general officers scarlet and staff officers crimson). Head-dress included the *burnous* for Arab units, but the regulation fez or fur tarboosh (*kalpac*) was usually replaced on active service by a distinctive greyish-khaki cloth helmet, styled a *kabalac* or *enverieh* ('Enver Pasha helmet'), originally a loose turban stitched into shape to produce a cloth sun-helmet, later amended by folding the cloth round a light, plaited straw framework. Its name was taken from Enver Pasha, who designed it (copied from the Italian sun-helmet) and who reputedly made a fortune from its patent. Supply of uniforms was spasmodic; Liman von Sanders recorded that during his inspections, the same uniforms were circulated around the units so that all would appear reasonably well-equipped upon his appearance; and the level of supply to the troops in the Gallipoli peninsula may be judged from the fact that when sandbags were issued to strengthen the defences, strict care had to be taken that these were not cut up to repair ragged uniforms! The principal weapon of the Turkish Army was the 7.65mm Mauser rifle, adopted in 1890, of the same calibre as the Belgian pattern but otherwise similar to the Spanish pattern of 1892.

The bulk of the Turkish Army was recruited from the peasantry of Anatolia and from the Arab inhabitants of the empire. The former were probably the army's most valuable resource: inured to a life of hardship which enabled them to survive upon the wretched rations allotted by the government, they were courageous and stubborn, which made them a formidable enemy. The quality of officer was low, those drawn from the ranks being especially poorly trained, despite the efforts of the German officers whose influence was great. (An exception was the body of 1,500 officers who had trained abroad, or under German instruction.) Shortages of ammunition had resulted in only limited rifle practise, so the standard of marksmanship was poor; yet the artillery was served competently. Initially, the Turk was regarded by the British as 'beastly' or an ignorant savage; experience of their combat capability in the Gallipoli campaign, however, changed that opinion to one of respect for the soldierly qualities of

▲ *'Abdul': a view of the Turkish soldier, drawn by Ted Colles of the 3rd Australian Light Horse*

Field Ambulance, published in The Anzac Book *(1916).*

'Johnny Turk', which respect was reciprocated.

From an establishment of some 200,000 enlisted men and 10,000 officers serving at the outbreak of war, mobilization of reservists had caused that total to rise to about one million by the end of 1914; yet the division of effort between the Caucasus, Middle East, Mesopotamia and the Dardanelles prevented a concentration of resources upon any one front, to the detriment of all.

Excluding *Goeben* and *Breslau*, the Turkish naval forces were negligible. The navy possessed two old battleships (*Häirredin Barbarousse* and *Torgud Reis*, built in 1891 and sold by Germany to Turkey in 1910, formerly the *Kurfürst Friedrich Wilhelm* and *Weissenburg* respectively), one coastal defence battleship of 1869 vintage (*Muin-i-Zaffer*, refitted in 1907 and armed with 6in guns), an armoured light cruiser (*Hamidieh*) and assorted destroyers, gun- and torpedo-boats. The other capital ship, the 1874 battleship *Messudieh*, rebuilt by Ansaldo of Genoa in 1902, had been sunk by the British submarine *B 11* on 13 December 1914. While one British description of this force as 'a weird collection of scrap-iron' is probably excessive, there was no possibility that the Turkish Navy could attempt to interfere in the campaign, and indeed it was incapable of preventing the depredations of Allied submarines that negotiated the Dardanelles.

The Allied Forces

In 1915 the British Army was still recruited by voluntary enlistment, units being divided into three basic categories. The regular regiments (those existing at full strength before the outbreak of war) were concentrated into regular divisions, and at this time still included a large proportion of experienced pre-war regular soldiers; the 29th Division, which served in the Dardanelles campaign, was almost exclusively 'regular' in composition (save one battalion of Territorials, the 5th Royal Scots). The second category comprised the

◀ *The field uniform of the British Army, worn by a member of the 8th Battalion, Lancashire Fusiliers, which served at Gallipoli as part of the 42nd Division. The cavalry-style bandolier and spurred boots identify him as a member of the battalion's transport section; the battalion-insignia (a white '8' upon a red diamond, worn at the shoulder) is clearly visible.*

Territorial battalions of regular regiments, part-time reservists; four of the Gallipoli divisions (42nd, 52nd–54th) were composed of these. The third category was the so-called 'New Army', newly created 'Service' battalions of the regular regiments, recruited almost entirely from those who had responded to Kitchener's appeals for volunteers; although they had a small professional cadre, both officers and men were completely inexperienced, though generally of very high morale. The 10th, 11th and 13th Divisions at Gallipoli were from the 'New Army'.

Divisional organization encompassed all necessary supporting services and artillery, though the heavier guns were normally assigned at corps or army level. Each infantry division comprised three brigades, each of four infantry battalions, with a squadron of cavalry and a cyclist company, two (later three) engineer companies, a signal company, three field ambulances and a divisional train of four companies of the Army Service Corps. Each infantry battalion had an establishment of about 1,000 of all ranks, with a combat strength of 800, organized into four rifle companies and a headquarters company. Divisional artillery consisted of three Field Brigades (18pdrs) and a Field Howitzer Brigade (4.5in howitzers), each with a Brigade Ammunition Column, supported by a Divisional Ammunition Column. At the outbreak of war a heavy battery of four 60pdrs might also be attached, which with 54 18pdrs and 18 howitzers gave a divisional total of 76 guns. By mid-1915, however, the usual divisional strength was 48 18pdrs and 8 howitzers, and some of the Territorial batteries had semi-obsolete 13pdrs. At the

▶ *Sergeant, Lancashire Fusiliers. This member of the battalion immortalized by 'Lancashire Landing' wears the universal khaki service dress of the British Army, initially with hardly any modifications for the climate, and the 1908-pattern webbing equipment. Throughout the ordinary infantry virtually the only differences in uniform were the insignia: here, the cap-badge of a brass grenade upon a white-metal title-scroll, and a brass grenade over the letters 'LF' on the shoulder-strap; on active service, such metalwork was allowed to tarnish. The cap might have ear-flaps or a neck-curtain, and when the wire stiffening was removed the resulting soft style was termed a 'Gorblimey'. The rifle is the S.M.L.E. (Short Magazine Lee-Enfield). (Painting by Cilla Eurich)*

◀ The most characteristic feature of the ANZAC uniform was the design of tunic and the felt slouch hat. This photograph of an anonymous 'digger' illustrates the use of the brass rising-sun badge, worn on the upturned brim of the hat and on the collar. The brass shoulder-title read 'AUSTRALIA'.

▶ A French regiment assembled with its colour-party in Egypt, prior to the landing at the Dardanelles. They wear the 'horizon-blue' field uniform introduced at the end of 1914, with horizon-blue covers on their kepis.

outbreak of war each battalion had two machine-guns, Maxims or Vickers; by mid-1915 this had risen to four Vickers guns each, giving a divisional total of 48 guns. At this date there were no independent machine-gun or trench-mortar units. By mid-1915 official divisional establishment was just over 18,000 men (all ranks), 5,000 horses, 834 vehicles and 54 motor vehicles.

The army wore the universal khaki field uniform with peaked cap introduced in 1902; the only major deviation from this was the kilt and head-dress of Highland regiments. The equipment was the khaki-green 1908-pattern webbing, and the standard firearm was the .303in Short Magazine Lee Enfield, of several 'Marks', a weapon capable of great accuracy and in the hands of a trained soldier of a rate-of-fire of 15 rounds per minute. Some concessions were made to the climate of the Mediterranean, in that some units were equipped with khaki topees and shorts, the latter often fabricated by cutting off the lower leg of the trousers; steel helmets were not used at this date. Other British formations serving as infantry at the Dardanelles included the 2nd Mounted Division of Yeomanry units, the Royal Naval Division of sailors and Royal Marines, and 29

Indian Brigade of the 1/5th, 1/6th and 2/10th Gurkha Rifles and the 14th Prince of Wales's Own Ferozepore Sikhs.

Forever associated with Dardanelles campaign will be the Australian and New Zealand Army Corps (ANZACs). The Australian Prime Minister, Andrew Fisher, declared that Australia would support Britain 'to the last man and the last shilling', and volunteers poured in to enlist. The existing Australian Army was a militia organization mainly of very young men, so a new army was created for overseas service, the Australian Imperial Forces (A.I.F.), organized in divisions on British lines. Equipment was generally like that of the British Army, but with tunics of khaki flannel which faded to grey-blue, plus the distinctive khaki felt slouch hat upturned at the left side. The New Zealand units wore basically the same style, their hats at this date generally like those of the Australians; the fashion to push the crown into the 'lemon-squeezer' style was introduced generally only after the Dardanelles campaign. Although the ANZAC forces were thus newly formed and inexperienced in combat, and despite what to British eyes appeared a grievous lack of discipline and respect for authority, their fighting qualities

were awesome. Combined with the resource-fulness and toughness often at the time attributed to 'colonials' used to an outdoor life, the resulting calibre of the ANZAC was probably never exceeded by any troops engaged in the war.

It is interesting to note that even a devastating level of casualties in British units did not result in their withdrawal from the line, though latterly temporary periods of rest were instituted. Instead, shattered units were amalgamated temporarily to produce a unit of practicable size from the wreck of two others. For example, in the 52nd Division on 6 July the 1/4th (Queen's Edinburgh Rifles) and 1/7th Royal Scots were formed into a composite battalion; within the 29th Division the 2nd Royal Fusiliers and Hampshire Regiment were joined (albeit belonging to different brigades), and the 1st Munster and 1st Royal Dublin Fusiliers were amalgamated to form a composite battalion styled 'the Dubsters' (by 4 May only *one* Dublins officer was not a casualty).

The French forces at the Dardanelles were composed of a mixture of 'metropolitan' (French) and colonial units, some regiments being an amalgamation of different services:

1st Division consisting of 1 Metropolitan Brigade (175th Regiment and a Composite Regiment of Zouaves and Foreign Legion) and a Colonial Brigade (4th and 6th Colonial Regiments)

2nd Division consisting of 2 Metropolitan Brigade (176th Regiment and 2nd African Regiment [Zouaves]) and a Colonial Brigade (7th and 8th Colonial Regiments)

The 'Colonial regiments' were composed partly of battalions of French colonial troops and partly of Senegalese. Each division included six field batteries armed with the superb *Soixante-Quinze* (75mm field-gun) and two mountain batteries. The French troops wore the service uniform of 'horizon blue' introduced at the end of 1914, though the colonial forces (including the Foreign Legion) wore the same style in light khaki (although at this time the Foreign Legion may have worn a mixture of khaki and light blue). Head-dress was either a kepi with horizon-blue or light khaki cover, or a khaki topee. Interestingly, a photograph of Zouaves on one of the Greek islands shows the old-style dark blue Zouave shirt and laced jacket, with white trousers and topee, but for the head-dress more like a costume from the Crimean War than from a modern campaign.

THE NAVAL ATTACK

Before the naval attack was instituted, Churchill asked the opinion of the officer commanding the Aegean, Vice-Admiral Sackville Carden. Carden stated that he believed the Dardanelles could be forced, given sufficient warships and mine-sweepers, in a three-stage plan; first a neutraliza-tion of the Turkish forts guarding the entrance, then a clearing of the Turkish minefields, and finally a drive into the Sea of Marmara. This persuaded the War Council to proceed, and despite Fisher's doubts, once his opposition was overcome (to the extent that he sanctioned the use of two more battleships, HMS *Lord Nelson* and, appropriately considering the historical setting of the Dardanelles, HMS *Agamemnon*), the plan was put into effect. In support, Kitchener authorized the transfer of the ANZACs to the Greek island of Lemnos, but prevaricated over the immediate dispatch of the 29th Division in case it should be required on the Western Front.

At no point from the entrance of the Darda-nelles to its junction with the Sea of Marmara was the channel out of range of the Turkish defences on both the European and Asiatic shores. At the mouth, the channel is 2¼ miles wide, guarded by the forts of Sedd-el-Bahr on the European side and Kum Kale on the Asiatic. Past these two fortifications the channel widens to some 4½ miles and then is reduced some fourteen miles upstream to 'the Narrows', less than a mile across, the

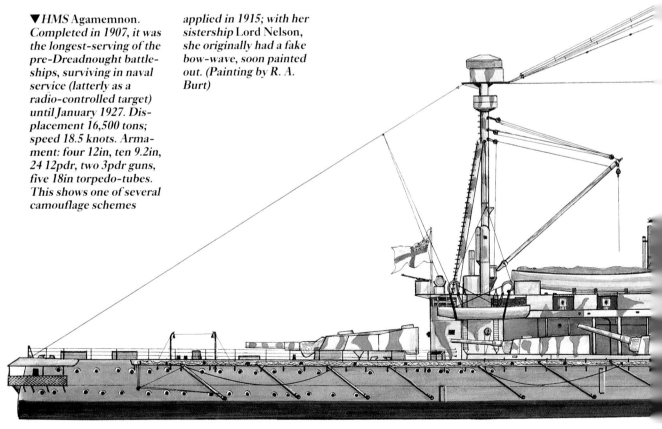

▼ *HMS* Agamemnon. *Completed in 1907, it was the longest-serving of the pre-Dreadnought battle-ships, surviving in naval service (latterly as a radio-controlled target) until January 1927. Dis-placement 16,500 tons; speed 18.5 knots. Arma-ment: four 12in, ten 9.2in, 24 12pdr, two 3pdr guns, five 18in torpedo-tubes. This shows one of several camouflage schemes* applied in 1915; with her sistership Lord Nelson, she originally had a fake bow-wave, soon painted out. (Painting by R. A. Burt)

location where Leander supposedly swam across. The approach was protected by the Kephez and Narrows minefields and a further pair of fortifications, Kilid Bahr on the European shore and Chanak Kale on the Asiatic. The main concentration of defences was at 'the Narrows', some 72 guns plus torpedo-tubes, but the most effective defences were 6in howitzer batteries deployed on both shores and capable of quite rapid movement. There were also searchlight batteries and latterly dummy batteries which emitted only smoke, serving to draw the fire of any attackers. Neutralization of both batteries and minefields was thus imperative, conducted with such speed as to preclude the reinforcement of the shore defences.

On 19 February Carden began his attack on the mouth of the Dardanelles, using twelve capital ships in three divisions, one French (Admiral Emile Guépratte with the battleships *Bouvet*, *Charlemagne*, *Gaulois* and *Suffren*) and two British, Carden himself in HMS *Queen Elizabeth*, with *Agamemnon* and *Inflexible*; and his deputy, Vice-Admiral Sir John de Robeck in HMS *Vengeance*, with *Albion*, *Cornwallis*, *Irresistible* and *Triumph*. The bombardment opened at long range, and although Carden sent in *Cornwallis*, *Vengeance* and *Suffren* much closer, hardly any opposing fire was drawn, and it was obvious that to silence the forts the fleet would need to close in and engage with observed fire. Bad weather prevented an immediate resumption of the operation, but on 25 February de Robeck led the fleet in a close-quarter attack; the defences were overpowered, the Turkish and German garrisons withdrew, and Allied landing-parties occupied Kum Kale and Sedd-el-Bahr, destroying the gun-positions. On 2

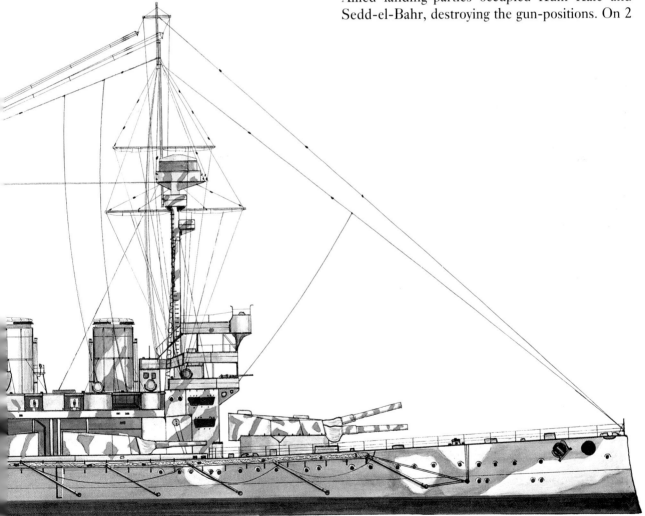

March Carden reported that he hoped to be through to Constantinople in about two weeks.

This was wildly optimistic. Returning to oppose the landings, the Turks caused the landing-parties to withdraw, and the mobile howitzer batteries proved too elusive to be destroyed by naval gunfire. The howitzers presented little danger to the battleships, but were formidable when bombarding the minesweepers, whose task of clearing the channel was the next stage in the Allied plan. The howitzers could not be opposed effectively by the fleet until the mines were cleared, and thus the minesweepers would be vulnerable when they made their initial attempt to clear the mines. The seaplanes, which should have acted as spotters to enable the fleet's gunnery to range on the shore-batteries, were constantly frustrated by weather conditions which prevented their taking off. Thus, it was perhaps not surprising that the minesweepers refused to go in; the vessels were small trawlers and their crews were civilians, who were not prepared to face artillery without protection. Commodore Roger Keyes, Carden's chief of staff, called for naval volunteers from the fleet to crew the minesweepers; but a determined attempt on 13 March, involving six trawlers and the cruiser *Amethyst*, ended when all but two of the trawlers were put out of action by the shore-batteries.

The constant delays prompted messages from Churchill to Carden, urging haste; these played upon Carden's nerves and on 15 March he announced that he could not go on, a doctor confirming his proximity to a nervous breakdown. Rear-Admiral Rosslyn E. Wemyss, commanding the base on Lemnos, was the senior officer in the area, but he willingly allowed de Robeck to take command of the fleet.

De Robeck made his main attack on 18 March 1915, in some respects a curious throwback. Unlike the great distances over which modern naval battles were fought, an observer on a high point on the shore could have seen the entire drama; as, in fact, did the Turkish and German artillery-spotters. In bright sunshine and without the possibility of surprise, de Robeck in HMS *Queen Elizabeth* led the first wave up the channel, towards the Kephez minefield, and began to pound the forts at Chanak Kale and Kilid Bahr at a distance of some eight miles; the forts were hardly able to reply, but the coastal and mobile batteries kept up an incessant fire, damaging the superstructure of some ships. The first wave included

ORDER OF BATTLE
The Naval Attack, 18 March 1915
(capital ships only)

Royal Navy: Vice-Admiral Sir John de Robeck

Queen Elizabeth: battleship, completed 1915. Armament: 8 × 15in; 16 × 6in; 2 × 3in

Agamemnon (1907): pre-Dreadnought battleship. Armament: 4 × 12in; 10 × 9.2in; 24 × 12pdr

Lord Nelson (1908): pre-Dreadnought battleship. Armament: as *Agamemnon*, but 15 × 12pdr

Irresistible (1902): *Formidable*-class pre-Dreadnought battleship. Armament: 4 × 12in; 12 × 6in; 18 × 12pdr

Vengeance (1901): *Canopus*-class pre-Dreadnought battleship. Armament: 4 × 12in; 12 × 6in; 12 × 12pdr

Ocean (1901): *Canopus*-class pre-Dreadnought battleship. Armament: as *Vengeance*

Inflexible (1908): *Invincible*-class battlecruiser. Armament: 8 × 12in; 16 × 4in

Swiftsure (1904): pre-Dreadnought battleship, ex-Chilean *Constitucion*. Armament: 4 × 10in; 14 × 7.5in; 14 × 14pdr

Triumph (1904): pre-Dreadnought battleship, ex-Chilean *Libertad*. Armament: as *Swiftsure*

Albion (1901): *Canopus*-class pre-Dreadnought battleship. Armament: 4 × 12in; 12 × 6in

Prince George (1896): *Majestic*-class pre-Dreadnought battleship. Armament: 4 × 12in; 12 × 6in; 16 × 12pdr

Majestic: (1895): pre-Dreadnought battleship. Armament: 4 × 12in; 12 × 6in; 18 × 12pdr

French Navy: Admiral Emile Guépratte (under de Robeck's command)

Bouvet (1898): battleship. Armament: 2 × 12in; 2 × 10.75in; 18 × 5.5in; 8 × 4in

Charlemagne (1899): battleship. Armament: 4 × 12in; 10 × 5.5in; 8 × 4in; 20 × 3pdr

Gaulois (1899): *Charlemagne*-class battleship. Armament: as *Charlemagne*

Suffren (1903): battleship. Armament: 4 × 12in; 10 × 6.4in; 8 × 4in; 22 × 3pdr

Reserve (support for minesweepers)

Canopus (1900): pre-Dreadnought battleship. Armament: as *Vengeance*.

Cornwallis (1904): pre-Dreadnought battleship. Armament: as *Vengeance*

▲ *A Turkish 10in gun destroyed at the fortifications of Sedd-el-Bahr.*

▶ *HMS* Inflexible *bombarding Turkish positions.*

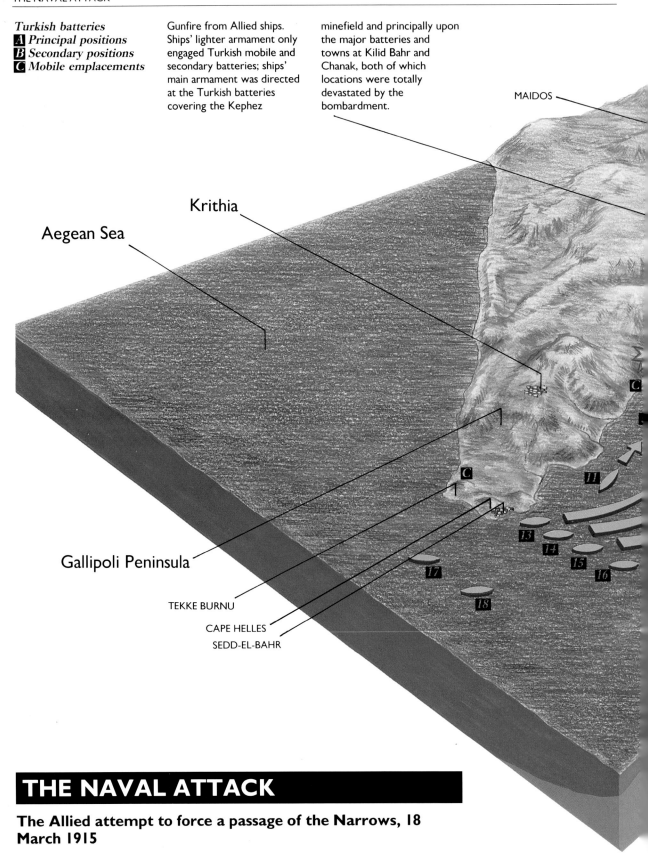

Turkish batteries
A Principal positions
B Secondary positions
C Mobile emplacements

Gunfire from Allied ships. Ships' lighter armament only engaged Turkish mobile and secondary batteries; ships' main armament was directed at the Turkish batteries covering the Kephez

minefield and principally upon the major batteries and towns at Kilid Bahr and Chanak, both of which locations were totally devastated by the bombardment.

MAIDOS

Krithia

Aegean Sea

Gallipoli Peninsula

TEKKE BURNU

CAPE HELLES

SEDD-EL-BAHR

THE NAVAL ATTACK

The Allied attempt to force a passage of the Narrows, 18 March 1915

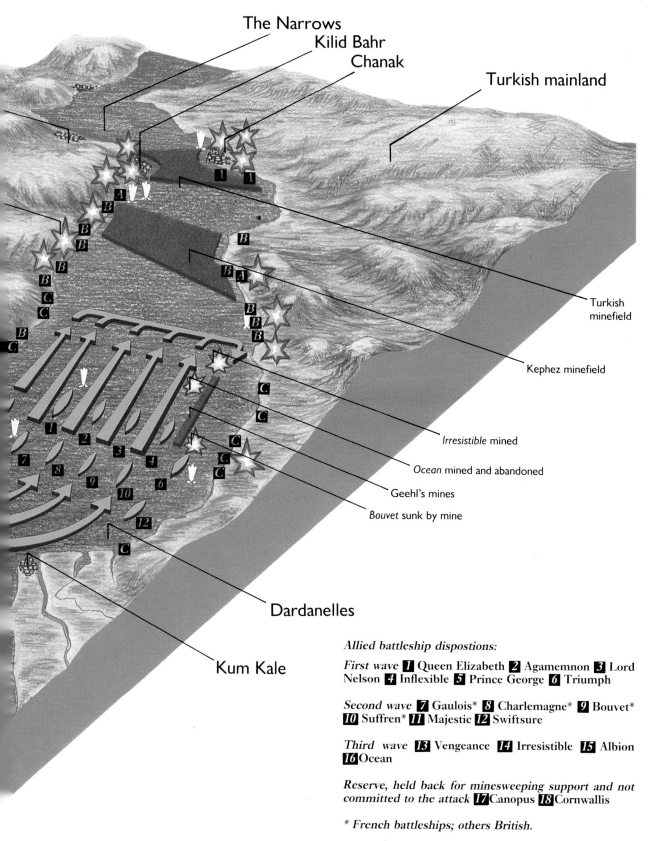

The Narrows

Kilid Bahr

Chanak

Turkish mainland

Turkish minefield

Kephez minefield

Irresistible mined

Ocean mined and abandoned

Geehl's mines

Bouvet sunk by mine

Dardanelles

Kum Kale

Allied battleship dispostions:

First wave **1** Queen Elizabeth **2** Agamemnon **3** Lord Nelson **4** Inflexible **5** Prince George **6** Triumph

Second wave **7** Gaulois* **8** Charlemagne* **9** Bouvet* **10** Suffren* **11** Majestic **12** Swiftsure

Third wave **13** Vengeance **14** Irresistible **15** Albion **16** Ocean

Reserve, held back for minesweeping support and not committed to the attack **17** Canopus **18** Cornwallis

* *French battleships; others British.*

◄ *The French battleship*
Bouvet, *sunk in the naval*
attack of 18 March with
the loss of almost all her
crew.

◄ *HMS* Ocean, *sunk in the*
naval attack of 18 March.

◄ *HMS* Irresistible *begins*
to sink during the naval
attack of 18 March.

de Robeck's four most powerful ships, *Queen Elizabeth* to pound the two forts at Chanak, *Agamemnon*, *Lord Nelson* and *Inflexible* to bombard Kilid Bahr; they were accompanied by *Prince George* on the European flank, and *Triumph* on the Asiatic. At midday, after 90 minutes' action, de Robeck signalled his second wave to go in closer, Guépratte's French squadron (*Bouvet*, *Charlemagne*, *Gaulois* and *Suffren*) with HMSS *Majestic* and *Swiftsure*.

Guépratte, so keen for action that he had specifically requested this mission, led his squadron through the British line and subjected the shore defences at the Narrows to an even fiercer bombardment, so that their fire almost died away. Shortly before 2 p.m. de Robeck signalled for the French to retire (*Gaulois* being holed below the waterline) and for his third wave to advance, HMSS *Albion*, *Irresistible*, *Ocean*, and *Vengeance*. Led by *Suffren*, the French ships turned towards the Asiatic shore to withdraw, and ran into an unknown menace. On 8 March a Turkish mine expert, Lieutenant-Colonal Geehl, had surreptitiously laid a line of twenty mines parallel to the Asiatic shore. Following immediately astern of *Suffren*, *Bouvet* hit a mine and within two minutes had disappeared entirely, with the loss of almost all her crew. Nevertheless, de Robeck's third wave (accompanied by *Majestic* and *Swiftsure*) came into action and, with the main Turkish guns virtually silenced, at about 4 p.m. six minesweepers were ordered forward. They cleared a few mines but then turned tail.

Then, *Inflexible* hit a mine not far from the grave of *Bouvet*. Despite severe damage, she kept afloat and limped out of the action. Shortly afterwards, *Irresistible* hit a mine; out of control, she was sufficiently near the Asiatic shore to attract the attention of Turkish gunners, and her crew was taken off by a destroyer. Unsure what had caused this damage (he suspected mines floated down the channel by the Turks), de Robeck abandoned the attack, but ordered Keyes to rescue the drifting *Irresistible*. Commanding from the destroyer HMS *Wear*, Keyes was given HMSS *Ocean* and *Swiftsure* for the task, but as the former's captain was unwilling to close in to tow the crippled ship, Keyes ordered *Ocean* to withdraw. Then, *Ocean* was riven by an explosion – probably another of Gheel's mines – and her steering gear was destroyed by a shell. Her crew was evacuated, and Keyes and *Swiftsure* withdrew. He returned after dark in the destroyer *Jed* in an attempt to sink *Irresistible* and, if possible, rescue *Ocean*; but both had sunk before he reached them.

Despite the losses, Keyes was convinced that the battle was won and that a renewed push would succeed. Very possibly it would have succeeded, for the Turkish guns had expended more than half their ammunition, including almost all of that for the heavier guns, the only ones capable of severely damaging battleships, and the towns at the Narrows were devastated. Even with the three lost ships, plus *Gaulois*, *Suffren* and *Inflexible* en route to Malta for repairs, a reinforcement of four British and two French battleships was on its way, and by Keyes' re-crewing of the trawlers and equipping destroyers with sweeping equipment, the force was substantially intact. Neither de Robeck nor Wemyss had full confidence in Keyes' assessment, being suspicious of his permanently offensive attitude, and the opinions of the military commanders were probably crucial in deciding de Robeck's course of action. Sir William Birdwood, commander of the ANZACs, had been present as an observer during Carden's command, and had reported to Kitchener at the beginning of March that a naval assault was unlikely to succeed. Sir Ian Hamilton arrived to command the military forces in time to witness the attack of 18 March, and may have influenced de Robeck. Whatever the case, as Kitchener was now prepared to use troops to force the Dardanelles, on 22 March de Robeck (who had been preparing for another naval attack) changed his mind and agreed with Hamilton: for the plan to succeed, the army would have to be used. The scheme now changed irrevocably from a naval to a military operation, and at the same time its chances of success had declined. It is easy to comment after the event, for the Allied commanders had no certain knowledge of the Turks' parlous state of ammunition; but had Keyes' urging been followed, it is very posssible that a victory could have been achieved by a renewed naval assault, and the troops spared the agony they were about to undergo.

▶ *HMS* Canopus, *a battleship built at Portsmouth Dockyard and completed in 1909; of the same class as* Goliath *and* Ocean, *both sunk during the Dardanelles campaign. Displacement 12,950 tons, capable of 18–19 knots.*

Armament: four 12in, twelve 6in, twelve 12pdr guns and four 18in torpedo tubes. Note here the short topmasts, searchlights on lower fighting-tops, and the mine-catcher mounted on the bow. Canopus *is shown in* a camouflage scheme as used in the Dardanelles campaign; this painting was not a success as the patterns tended to merge at a distance of several thousand yards. (Painting by R. A. Burt)

▼ *HMS* Inflexible, *a battlecruiser completed in 1908. The concept of the battlecruiser was to create a vessel with almost the hitting-power of a battleship but much greater speed, which necessitated much lighter armour (6in, turrets 7in); battlecruisers were also longer and had more powerful engines. Displacement 17,250 tons, speed 25–6 knots. Armament: eight 12in, sixteen 4in guns, five 18in torpedo-tubes. (The wing turret arrangement was such that it limited broadsides to six 12in guns, a feature remedied in succeeding designs of battlecruisers.)* Inflexible *was mined during the campaign but remained afloat and survived to fight at Jutland. She was sold for scrap in December 1921. (Painting by R. A. Burt)*

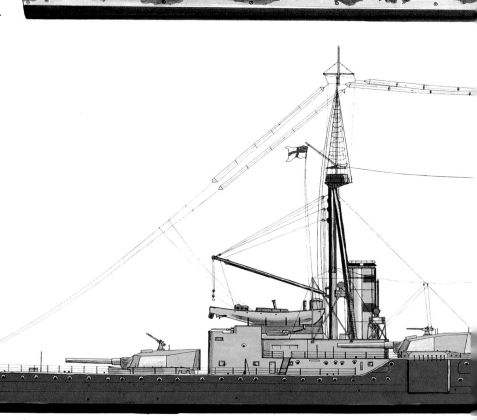

THE LANDINGS

Churchill drafted a signal to de Robeck ordering an immediate resumption of the naval attack, but after discussion with the Admiralty, the signal was never sent: Fisher was adamant that the judgement of the admiral on the spot should be respected, and although Prime Minister Herbert H. Asquith (head of the War Council) said he supported Churchill, he would not oppose the naval opinion. Kitchener declared that the army was prepared to shoulder the burden, so events were put in motion for one of the costliest blunders of the war.

Confusion reigned from the beginning. There was no supreme commander, military and naval forces remaining under independent leadership (not really the fault of the War Council at the outset, for a 'combined operation' had not been envisaged); Intelligence was very poor, for the detailed files assembled before the war were never consulted; and planning for the military operation was lamentable. Greek islands were to be used as bases for the landings, but little thought had been given to improving their facilities. Lemnos had a large natural harbour, but little capacity for disembarking troops and supplies, and inadequate water, so that many troops were dispersed over other Aegean islands, or remained in the troopships. The loading of equipment and supplies had been haphazard, and the scattering of units around the Aegean made a concerted action impossible. Hamilton had therefore to reorganize his army, which could only be done in Egypt; so he departed for Alexandria, telling de Robeck that he would return in mid-April. Whatever chance of surprise

might have existed was thus lost, and the period between the battle of 18 March and the eventual military descent was put to good use by Liman von Sanders, appointed to command by Enver on the day that Hamilton left for Alexandria.

Liman von Sanders found the defenders of the Gallipoli peninsula arrayed along the coast in such a manner that had a break been made in their defence-line the Allies could have rolled them up, there being no organization of a reserve. He immediately amended their dispositions. His force consisted of some 80,000 men in six divisions, collectively styled the Fifth Army. Two divisions (3rd and 11th) he stationed on the Asiatic coast south of Kum Kale, where he believed the main threat to lie. On the Gallipoli peninsula were four practicable landing-sites (excluding those on the eastern shore which, being overlooked by the Turkish defences on the Asiatic shore, were obviously out of the question for sites of an Allied landing). At the north of the peninsula was Bulair; Liman von Sanders posted his 7th Division in the Bulair/Gallipoli area, with 5th Division to its north-east, covering the Gulf of Saros. The other three possible landing-areas were at Suvla, midway on the western shore of the peninsula; Ari Burnu, farther south; and at Cape Helles, the tip of the peninsula. Importantly for defence, each was overlooked by high ground: Achi Baba hill to the north of Helles, the Sari Bair ridge at Ari Burnu, and Tekke Tepe ridge overlooking Suvla. Liman von Sanders posted his 9th Division at Cape Helles, around Krithia; and his final division, the 19th under Mustafa Kemal, he located as a mobile reserve at Maidos and Boghali to the north of the Narrows, ready to reinforce either the troops at Bulair, the Asiatic shore, or Helles, depending on where the Allies landed. Liman von Sanders then began a period of intensive training, erected such defences as he could before supplies of barbed

◀ *Top Left: Troops rowed ashore by boats on the day of the initial landing.*

◀ *The landing of the 4th (New South Wales) Battalion, 4 Australian Brigade, at Anzac Cove at*

about 8 a.m. on 25 April. The staff of 1 Brigade are assembled in the foreground; one of the first Gallipoli casualties lies dead on the shoreline. (Australian War Memorial, neg. no. A 1090)

37

wire ran out, and constructed land-mines from torpedo-heads. The time he gained by Hamilton's need to reorganize in Egypt was vital.

Having improved the harbour facilities at Lemnos, Hamilton prepared for two landings: the ANZACs to disembark at Ari Burnu (designated as 'Z' Beach) and the remainder around the tip of the peninsula, on five beaches designated: 'S', 'V', 'W', 'X' and 'Y'. This Helles landing was entrusted largely to the superb 29th Division, which

The Dardanelles: Turkish defenses

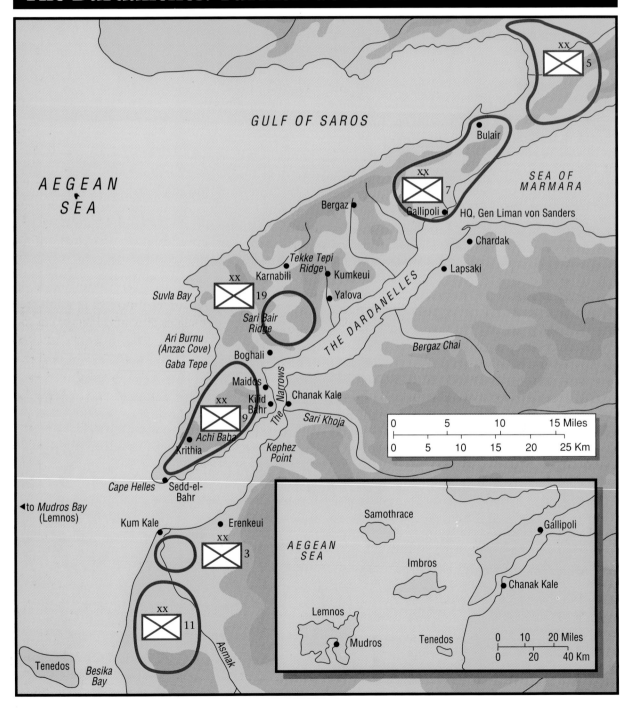

finally had been released by Kitchener; and the French were to land on the Asiatic coast around Kum Kale. The total strength of Hamilton's force comprised the British 29th and Royal Naval Divisions (17,600 and 10,000 men respectively); 1st Australian and Australian and New Zealand Divisions (30,500 total), the latter including 29 Indian Brigade; and 16,700 French under the command of General Albert d'Amade. Simultaneously, it was planned that the Royal Naval Division was to make a diversionary landing at Bulair, which, like the French descent on Kum Kale, was to be withdrawn and the troops added to the main landings once their job of confusing the Turks had been accomplished.

That the main landing-site was the Gallipoli peninsula was obvious: had the main landings been at Bulair on Kum Kale, the Allied army would have been open to attack from the rear as they progressed inland, and would have lost the covering-fire of the fleet. There was even merit in the dispersal of forces over six beaches plus two diversions: initially Liman von Sanders would not know which was the main landing, and thus could not concentrate fully to oppose any one. The invasion-force was to assemble at Mudros harbour on the island of Lemnos, with smaller bases established on Tenedos, Imbros and Skyros; for the actual landing the army would be transferred from troopships to lighters and similar small craft, to be towed ashore in strings of four by motor-launches, there being no specifically designed landing-craft. At 'V' Beach, some 2,000 men were to be landed from a 1905 collier, SS *River Clyde*, purchased in April 1915, which was to be run aground, with the troops disembarking through doors cut in the ship's sides, on to lighters lashed to her bow to form a bridge to shore. The whole operation was to be possibly the greatest amphibious landing ever attempted, far bigger that that made by the British in Egypt in 1801, and different from the Crimea in that the landing would be opposed. The objectives for the initial landing were: to establish a wide bridgehead at Ari Burnu and to occupy the entire tip of the Helles peninsula, extending to the north-east of Krithia and taking the vital high ground overlooking the beaches. Surprisingly, given the confusion at other

stages of the campaign, the fleet was assembled without difficulty; the landing was scheduled for dawn on Sunday, 25 April, the troops carrying only light equipment, ammunition, and three days' rations.

It is interesting at this stage to compare the conduct of the commanders. Ian Hamilton positioned himself in *Queen Elizabeth*, and so had no way of appreciating the situation on the beaches, behaviour he was to repeat throughout the campaign and which has attracted much criticism. Being so far removed, he left the actual operations to his subordinates, the competent Birdwood at Ari Burnu (henceforth referred to as Anzac Cove, or just 'Anzac'), and the excessively optimistic and immeasurably less capable Sir Aylmer Hunter-Weston at Helles. The lack of a strong, guiding hand was a fatal flaw in the Allies' campaign. Liman von Sanders was not present to oversee the defence against the landings; believing that the Bulair diversion was the main offensive, he remained in the north even after he had received reports of the landings at Helles and Anzac, but on the following day diverted the bulk of the two Bulair divisions to the south, and took command in person. Despite his absence and lack of reinforcement (save five battalions dispatched by Liman von Sanders from Gallipoli to the Narrows on first learning of the southern landings), the Turkish defenders fought with amazing tenacity and were as responsible for the lack of Allied progress as was the confusion in the Allied command.

For the landings of 25 April, each will be taken in order, from south to north and around the Helles tip of the peninsula.

ANZAC

The Ari Burnu area to be assaulted by the ANZACs was the least well reconnoitered of the landing-beaches, and hemmed by precipitous cliffs, a terrible, inhospitable landscape. To oppose 3 Australian Brigade which made the first landfall was the 2nd Battalion of the Turkish 27th Regiment, with a mountain battery to the north of, and four 15cm guns to the south of, Gaba Tepe headland. The ANZACs landed from their small boats without mishap in the early dawn on 25

April; desultory rifle-fire came from the coast but the beaches were cleared by the bayonet. Instead of the expected wide beach of easy access, impossible terrain was encountered, cliffs and gullies covered with scrub, exceptionally difficult to climb. Daylight revealed that instead of landing at 'Z' Beach, the first troops had been deposited farther north, at Ari Burnu itself; the boats had been swept more than a mile north by an unexpected current. As the main Turkish defenders and the 15cm guns were to the south at Gaba Tepe, although they could sweep the expected landing-beaches, the area in which the ANZACs had actually landed was defended very weakly, and thus isolated parties were able to progress so far inland that they could actually look across the peninsula to the Narrows; but so difficult was the terrain that a co-ordinated advance was impossible, and the many isolated skirmishes were fought largely without direction or support. After some delay, 3 Brigade was followed by 2 Brigade (with an Indian mountain battery); 1 Brigade was ashore and in action before noon, followed by the New Zealand and 4 Brigades.

Into this confused fighting came Mustafa Kemal, commanding 19th Division at Boghali. He moved towards the landing in early morning, a difficult march over precipitous terrain, and immediately appreciated the strategic implications: that the vital features were not the beaches but the Sari Bair ridge and Chunuk Bair mount, possession of which might decide the campaign. Had the ANZACs been able to establish themselves on this eminence before the Turks could react, they would have dominated the whole central portion of the peninsula. Without authority, Kemal ordered up all the forces he could muster, and in late morning returned to corps headquarters to request even more of the reserve. Essad Pasha, his corps commander, had no choice but to concede, and from this moment Kemal was actually in command of the entire defence against the ANZAC landing. The Turkish counter-attack stabilized their position in very confused and most bitter fighting among the gullies and broken ground, an unrelenting struggle which lasted throughout the day, and enabled the Turks to prevent the capture of the Sari Bair ridge; and, thus, quite possibly, decided the outcome of the campaign.

'Y' Beach

Four miles up the coast from Cape Helles, the landing at 'Y' Beach was conceived by Hamilton as an attempt to take the Turkish defenders of the cape in the rear; 2,000 men deposited at this isolated spot could march across the peninsula, roll up the defenders and join the troops landed at Cape Helles. It was not actually a beach as such, but a 200-foot cliff; but it was entirely undefended.

◀ *The landing at dawn, 25 April: the battleship* Implacable *(four 12in, twelve 6in, eighteen 12pdr guns) bombards the shore; on the horizon at the extreme right are boats towed by pinnaces, taking the 2nd Royal Fusiliers towards 'X' Beach.*

▶ *Trawlers were used in the campaign both as minesweepers and for transport: this vessel is packed with members of the 6th Lancashire Fusiliers (42nd Division), moving from their transport, SS* Nile, *to the landing-beaches.*

(A verse appeared in the newspaper *Dardanelles Driveller* on 17 May which described the position:

> '"Y" Beach, the Scottish Borderer cried
> While panting up the steep hillside,
>   "Y" Beach!
> To call this thing a beach is stiff,
> It's nothing but a b----- cliff.
>   Why "beach"?')

The cliffs were climbed without hindrance, but such was the confusion in orders that neither of the unit COs involved knew who was senior and thus in command, and neither appreciated the significance of their position. Consequently, the 1st King's Own Scottish Borderers and Plymouth Battalion, Royal Marines sat serenely upon the cliff-top all day, doing nothing while their comrades were being slaughtered on the other beaches. Twice the 'Y' Beach commanders asked Hunter-Weston for orders, but received no reply. Hamilton sailed past in *Queen Elizabeth* and Keyes begged him to put more men ashore there – the Royal Naval Division could have been landed before dark once their Bulair demonstration had ended – but Hamilton, though appreciating the tactical significance, felt that he could not issue such orders without the approval of Hunter-Weston! The latter had to be signalled twice before he replied, and then said that to land more troops at 'Y' Beach would delay disembarkation on

the other beaches. Lieutenant-Colonel Matthews of the Marines actually walked to Krithia and the hill of Achi Baba, which were entirely deserted; but without official approval no attempt was made to occupy these vital positions which, if taken that day, might have decided the campaign and certainly avoided untold slaughter in the succeeding months.

'W' and 'X' Beaches

The landings on 'V', 'W' and 'X' Beaches were largely entrusted to 29th Division's 86 Brigade of four fusilier battalions. Their commander, Brigadier-General S.W. Hare, quoted regimental tradition in an order exhorting his men to behave, ' . . . in such a way that the men of Albuhera and Minden, of Delhi and Lucknow may hail us as their equals in valour and military achievement'. His troops were accommodated in *Implacable* and *Euryalus*, before being decanted into boats towed by steam-pinnaces; heavy naval covering-fire was provided. 'X' Beach consisted of a 200-yard strip of sand with a 40-foot escarpment, easily negotiable by infantry but difficult for artillery, which is probably why the Turks had made so few preparations: 'X' Beach had but twelve defenders when the 2nd Royal Fusiliers waded ashore from their boats. This battalion easily gained a lodgement and attempted to join their comrades by pushing towards 'W' Beach, but high ground in the intervening mile was held by Turks and some shellfire was directed upon them; but reinforced by the succeeding wave (1st Inniskilling Fusiliers and 1st Border Regiment of 87 Brigade.) they pushed on and before dark linked up with 'W' Beach.

Opposition was infinitely greater on 'W' Beach. Two companies of the Turkish 2/26th Regiment covered 'W' and 'V' Beaches, fortified with wire and machine-guns, and these laid down a barrage of fire into the 1st Lancashire Fusiliers who landed mostly in boats from *Euryalus*. The action which resulted has passed into the folklore of the county: of the men wading ashore, 'mown down as by a scythe' as Hamilton stated, winning in the process 'six VCs before breakfast'. Despite severe casualties, the Fusiliers struggled through the wire in an operation described by Hamilton as unsurpassed in British military annals, and sup-

▶ *The 6th Lancashire Fusiliers en route to the landing beaches. They wear the ordinary service uniform plus the topee, the latter bearing regimental insignia on the left side of a scarlet patch with a white grenade over 'LF'.*

▼ *'Lancashire Landing': the 1st Lancashire Fusiliers fight their way ashore on 'W' Beach. The officer with the cane (centre) is Captain Richard Raymond Willis, one of the battalion's six VCs. (Print after S. Begg)*

The Landings, 25 April 1915

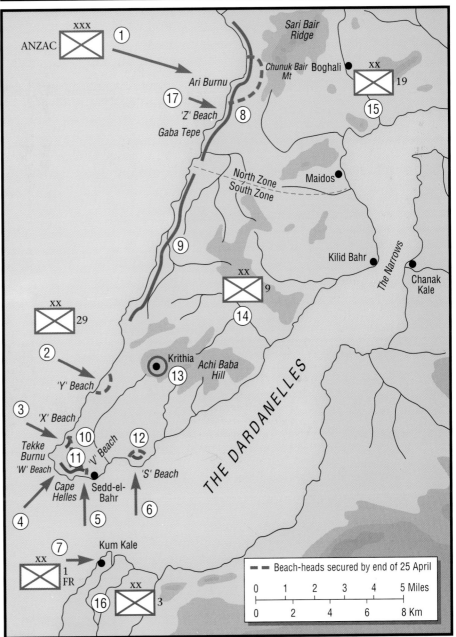

▶ Unit positions:
1. ANZAC Corps: initial landing by 3 Bde., followed by 2 and 1 Bdes. (all 1st Australian Div.); then New Zealand Bde. and 4 Bde. (both Australian and New Zealand Div.)
Landings of 29th Division:
2. 'Y' Beach, 1/K.O.S.B. (87 Bde.), Plymouth Btn. R.M. (R.N. Div.)
3. 'X' Beach, 2/R. Fusiliers (86 Bde.), followed by 1/Border Regt.., 1/R. Inniskilling Fusiliers (both 87 Bde.)
4. 'W' Beach, 1/Lancashire Fusiliers (86 Bde.), followed by 4/Worcestershire Regt. (88 Bde.)
5. 'V' Beach, 1/R. Munster Fusiliers, 1/R. Dublin

Fusiliers (both 86 Bde.), part 2/Hampshire Regt. (88 Bde.)
6. 'S' Beach, 2/S. Wales Borderers (87 Bde.)
7. landing of French 1st Division, Kum Kale: initially 6th Colonial Regt.
Location of Turkish units:
8. 3 companies 27th Regt., covering Ari Burnu/Gaba

Tepe area
9. 3 companies 26th Regt., between Gaba Tepe and Sari Tepe
10. 1 section, 26th Regt. (12 men), covering 'X' Beach
11. 2 companies 26th Regt., covering 'W' and 'V' Beaches
12. 1 platoon, 26th Regt., covering 'S' Beach
13. Headquarters 26th

Regt. (total 2 battns., 1 engineer coy.), Krithia
14. Reserve, 9th Division (2 battns. 25th Regt.)
15. Reserve, 19th Division at Boghali (8 battns.)
16. 3rd Division (part), Kum Kale
17. Intended 'Z' Beach at Anzac; troops landed by error at Ari Burnu.

◀River Clyde at 'V' Beach, with supplies being transferred to shore. Clearly visible here are the sandbagged machine-gun nests in her bows, which engaged the Turks throughout 25 April.

▼The River Clyde showing the bridge of boats running from her bows to shore. The sally-ports cut in the sides of the hull through which the troops exited are clearly visible as dark rectangles.

ported by the 4th Worcesters from 88 Brigade held their bridgehead. It is noteworthy that the Turks did not open fire until the troops were actually landing; no attempt was made to strafe the unprotected boats, perhaps to avoid revealing their positions and attracting shellfire from the fleet, or perhaps to prevent the attack from being postponed and thus losing the opportunity of trapping the British on the beach. As a testimony to the gallantry of the troops, Hamilton ordered 'W' Beach to be known as 'Lancashire Landing'.

'V' Beach

Together with Lancashire Landing, probably the most enduring image of the initial landings is the attack from the *River Clyde*. At first light the battleship *Albion* bombarded the Turkish positions for an hour, whereupon the collier was run aground; she had aboard the 1st Royal Munster Fusiliers, two companies of the 2nd Hampshire Regiment and one of the 1st Royal Dublin Fusiliers, and a field company of Royal Engineers.

ORDER OF BATTLE
The Initial Landing, 25 April 1915
(principal units only)

29th Division

86 Brigade: 2/Royal Fusiliers; 1/Lancashire Fusiliers; 1/Royal Munster Fusiliers; 1/Royal Dublin Fusiliers

87 Brigade: 2/South Wales Borderers; 1/King's Own Scottish Borderers; 1/Royal Inniskilling Fusiliers; 1/Border Regiment

88 Brigade: 2/Hampshire Regiment; 4/Worcestershire Regiment; 1/Essex Regiment; 5/Royal Scots

Royal Naval Division

1 Naval Brigade: Drake, Nelson and Deal (Royal Marine) Battalions

2 Naval Brigade: Howe, Hood and Anson Battalions

3 Marine Brigade: Chatham, Portsmouth and Plymouth Battalions

(Progressive changes in division included the addition of Hawke, Benbow and Collingwood Battalions; 2 and 3 Brigades amalgamated 2 August, and marine battalions amalgamated 12 August to form 1st and 2nd Marine Battalions)

1st Australian Division

1 Australian Brigade: 1st–4th New South Wales Battalions

2 Australian Brigade: 5th–8th Victoria Battalions

3 Australian Brigade: 9th Queensland; 10th S. Australian; 11th W. Australian, 12th S. & W. Australian and Tasmanian Battalion

Divisional troops: 4th Victorian Light Horse

Australian and New Zealand Division

4 Australian Brigade: 13th New South Wales; 14th Victoria; 15th Queensland & Tasmania; 16th S. & W. Australian Battalions

New Zealand Infantry Brigade: Auckland, Canterbury, Wellington and Otago Battalions

1 Australian Light Horse Brigade: 1st New South Wales; 2nd Queensland; 3rd South Australian and Tasmanian Regiments

1st French Division

1 Metropolitan Brigade: 175th Regiment; Composite Regiment of Zouaves and Foreign Legion

Colonial Brigade: 4th and 6th Colonial Regiments

(Only principal units are listed; in addition, each division had the usual complement of artillery and supporting services.)

---

soon as *River Clyde* grounded, shortly before 6.30 a.m., a storm of fire erupted from the Turks, who had returned to their trenches after the bombardment ended. A few men disembarked from the boats and ran to shelter under a bank at the side of the cliff; the remainder were mown down by fire so hot that it proved impossible to get the lighters into position to act as the bridge from the collier to the beach. The armour-plated sides of *River Clyde* were proof against the fire, but the troops were marooned inside. The sea at 'V' Beach became red with blood as far out as fifty yards from shore.

By 9.30 a.m. it was obvious that the position was hopeless, with scarcely 200 men established on the beach; but Hunter-Weston, aboard *Euryalus* and without making inquiries as to the progress of the landing, ordered in the succeeding wave. Too few of the landing-boats were still operational for the second wave to be sacrificed, but their commander, Brigadier-General Napier of 88 Brigade, was killed attempting to reach the beach. A renewed attempt to break out of *River Clyde* only increased the number of troops on the beach to about 400, and not until darkness did the survivors file off the shot-riddled ship, this time without sustaining a casualty.

'S' Beach

The landing by the 2nd South Wales Borderers (87 Brigade), a party from *Cornwallis* and an engineer detachment was accomplished with great success, proof of what might have been achieved elsewhere with better planning. Landing later than the rest at 7.30 a.m., by 10 a.m. the Borderers had captured the main defences, then dug in and repulsed whatever counter-attacks were made. Here, unlike the other beaches, the Turkish trenches were visible from the sea, and so the covering naval bombardment was of greater significance.

Kum Kale

The French landing at Kum Kale was partly diversionary, and partly to prevent artillery fire upon the British landings across the channel. The operation was covered by three French battleships

The remainder of the Dublins landed by picket-boat, with a half-company going in east of Seddel-Bahr; they were unable to break through to the main landing and the survivors were evacuated. As

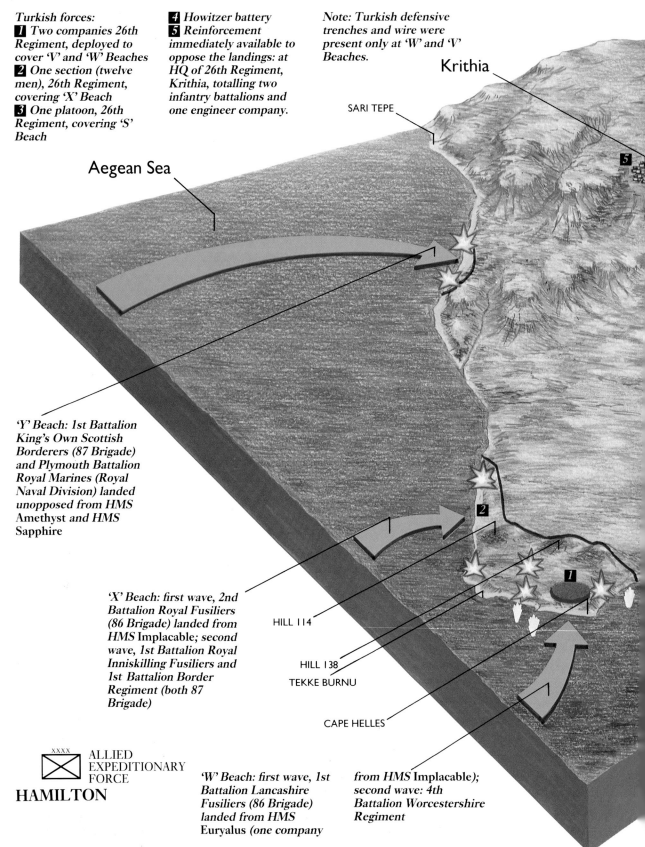

Turkish forces:

1 Two companies 26th Regiment, deployed to cover 'V' and 'W' Beaches
2 One section (twelve men), 26th Regiment, covering 'X' Beach
3 One platoon, 26th Regiment, covering 'S' Beach

4 Howitzer battery
5 Reinforcement immediately available to oppose the landings: at HQ of 26th Regiment, Krithia, totalling two infantry battalions and one engineer company.

Note: Turkish defensive trenches and wire were present only at 'W' and 'V' Beaches.

Krithia

SARI TEPE

Aegean Sea

'Y' Beach: 1st Battalion King's Own Scottish Borderers (87 Brigade) and Plymouth Battalion Royal Marines (Royal Naval Division) landed unopposed from HMS Amethyst and HMS Sapphire

'X' Beach: first wave, 2nd Battalion Royal Fusiliers (86 Brigade) landed from HMS Implacable; second wave, 1st Battalion Royal Inniskilling Fusiliers and 1st Battalion Border Regiment (both 87 Brigade)

HILL 114

HILL 138

TEKKE BURNU

CAPE HELLES

XXXX
ALLIED EXPEDITIONARY FORCE

HAMILTON

'W' Beach: first wave, 1st Battalion Lancashire Fusiliers (86 Brigade) landed from HMS Euryalus (one company from HMS Implacable); second wave: 4th Battalion Worcestershire Regiment

THE LANDING AT CAPE HELLES

'S', 'V', 'W', 'X' and 'Y' Beaches, 25 April 1915

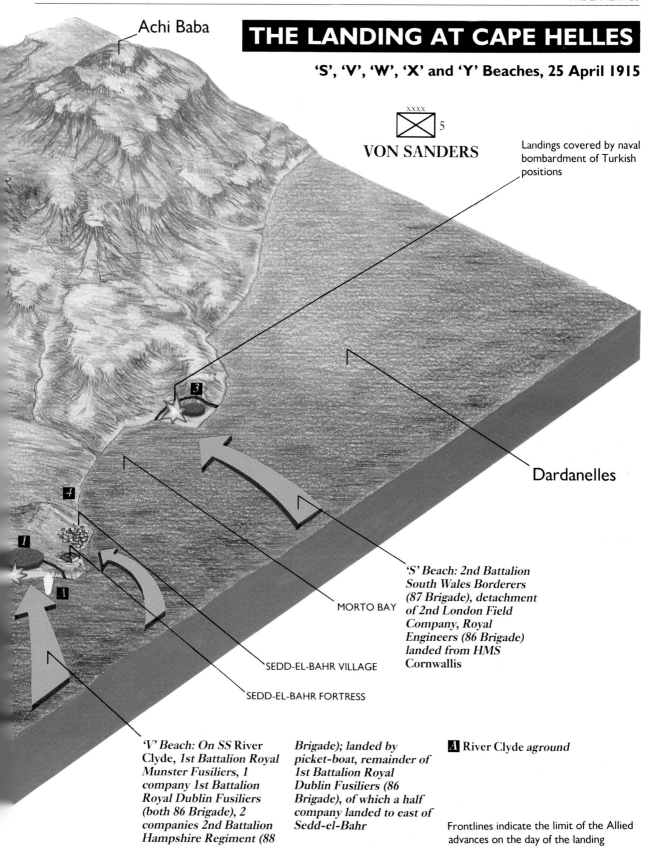

VON SANDERS

Landings covered by naval bombardment of Turkish positions

Achi Baba

Dardanelles

MORTO BAY

SEDD-EL-BAHR VILLAGE

SEDD-EL-BAHR FORTRESS

'S' Beach: 2nd Battalion South Wales Borderers (87 Brigade), detachment of 2nd London Field Company, Royal Engineers (86 Brigade) landed from HMS Cornwallis

'V' Beach: On SS River Clyde, 1st Battalion Royal Munster Fusiliers, 1 company 1st Battalion Royal Dublin Fusiliers (both 86 Brigade), 2 companies 2nd Battalion Hampshire Regiment (88 Brigade); landed by picket-boat, remainder of 1st Battalion Royal Dublin Fusiliers (86 Brigade), of which a half company landed to east of Sedd-el-Bahr

4 River Clyde aground

Frontlines indicate the limit of the Allied advances on the day of the landing

◀ *French artillery being towed towards shore on a lighter, near Sedd-el-Bahr.*

◀ *The Russian cruiser Askold, completed 1903, armed with twelve 6in, twelve 12pdr, eight 3pdr and two 1pdr guns.*

◀ *Part of the Allied armada photographed off Helles shortly after the landing, showing a Turkish wire entanglement in the foreground.*

◀ Headquarters of the 2nd Royal Fusiliers on the cliffs above 'X' Beach, shortly after landing on 25 April. The officer in profile (left) is the battalion's commanding officer, Lieutenant-Colonel Newenham, who was wounded later that day; next to him, facing the camera, is the Adjutant, Captain Thomas Duncombe Shafto, who was killed on 2 May.

(*Henri IV, Jeanne d'Arc* and *Jauréguiberry*) and the one Russian ship in the fleet, the cruiser *Askold* (known throughout the expedition as 'the packet of Woodbines' from the appearance of its five thin funnels!). The first wave consisted of the 6th Colonial Regiment and an engineer detachment, and although the boats covered by *Askold* came under fire at sea and had to make off, the remainder landed and secured the fort and village of Kum Kale. After reinforcement they held on against a counter-attack by the Turkish 3rd Division.

Consolidation

Despite many failings, notably the inactivity and ignorance of the actual situation among the higher command, the lodgement had been made and was held on all but 'Y' Beach. This landing ended as it had begun, in confusion. Towards the evening of 25 April a Turkish attack was launched from the north, and continued all night. The British had not bothered to entrench properly, and after the death of Colonel Koe of the King's Own Scottish Borderers his half of the landing-force requested evacuation, which the navy accomplished. The Marine commander, Colonel Matthews, initially unaware that half the position had been abandoned, thus had no option but to withdraw despite having driven off a renewed Turkish attack on the early morning of 26 April. Ironically, at this moment the Turks also thought they had been beaten and retired, enabling Matthews' detachment to get away without further loss, demonstrating what a shambles the entire 'Y' Beach landing had been.

The operation had been hindered by the restricted number of landing-vessels available; at Anzac, for example, the Australasian Corps had only the capacity to transport 1,500 men at a time, and although the rate of disembarkation was speeded by the use of destroyers and trawlers which were able to approach near to shore, reinforcements could only be fed in comparatively slowly. The fleet had provided covering fire when it could, but communications with the shore were so bad that often they dare not fire for fear of hitting their own troops. Worst of all was the lack of direction, neither Hamilton nor Hunter-Weston being able to judge the true state of the position. Nevertheless, almost 30,000 troops had been disembarked, despite fearful casualties, and at Helles the Turks were shattered, having lost half of the 2,000 men who had opposed the landings. A determined push from the beaches during the night could well have achieved the landings' initial territorial objectives; but the paralysis of the central command continued.

The situation at Anzac, however, was critical. Kemal's counter-attacks had been mounted with

such vigour that the ANZAC forward positions had been lost, and the error in landing meant that instead of a beach a mile long, the corps had barely half that, only thirty yards wide, creating impossible congestion upon the small jetty which had been built following the landing. The defenders were penned into a bridgehead less than 3,500 yards long by about 1,200 yards deep, in broken terrain, the troops exhausted, disorganized and in need of food and water. Unlike his opposite number at Helles, Birdwood had been ashore all the afternoon, and was recalled by his divisional commanders who insisted that the beachhead be evacuated, as their forces were incapable of resisting a renewed Turkish assault. (In fact, Kemal had suffered 2,000 casualties and was in no position to launch a major counter-attack.) Birdwood signalled to Hamilton that his position was critical and that his subordinates had advised evacuation. Hamilton was unsure how to reply, but news that the Australian submarine *AE 2* had slipped through the Narrows into the Sea of Marmara (where it was eventually captured) he took as an omen. He replied to Birdwood that Hunter-Weston's eventual attack would relieve the pressure, and that all the ANZACs had to do was to dig, dig, dig, and 'stick it out'. That the Australasians were able to do this after what they had suffered is sufficient testimony of their determination. The term 'diggers' may originally have been accorded to Australians from the gold-mining of the previous century; but after Gallipoli, Diggers they would be for ever.

◀ *This ANZAC wears the Australian field uniform, based upon the British equivalent but with a distinctive tunic of drab or khaki flannel, which faded to its original blue-grey colour, with plain buttons and voluminous pockets. The khaki felt hat was the most distinctive item of uniform and bore upon the upturned flap the same insignia as often carried upon the collar, the bronzed metal 'rising sun' badge of the Aus-* *tralian Imperial Forces. The shoulder-strap did not usually bear battalion identification, but instead the brass title 'Australia'. Weaponry and equipment was like that of the British Army. (Painting by Cilla Eurich)*

▶ *Anzac Cove: divisional headquarters staff land from ships' boats. (Australian War Memorial, neg. no G 903)*

▶ *A supply-launch sunk by Turkish gunfire off one of the makeshift piers built at Anzac.*

▶ *Turkish prisoners are interrogated by British officers. Note the shorts worn by the prisoners' escorts (left), and the neck-curtain worn by the officer with the cap.*

THE BATTLES OF KRITHIA

Hamilton's command to dig set the tone for the remainder of the campaign. Henceforth, the troops at both bridgeheads existed in dugouts scraped in the earth, and in the firing-line trenches and outposts were similarly excavated in those positions where the terrain was at all suitable for digging. Initially there were few thoughts of prolonged existence under such conditions, but such was the inevitable consequence of Hamilton's order to dig, testimony that the element of surprise had been lost, and that what followed was little different in essence from the static trench-warfare of the Western Front.

The first priorities for the attackers were the evacuation of casualties (which had caused great congestion and had slowed the initial reinforcement at Anzac) and to feed in supplies, especially artillery, the lack of which had been a severe handicap to the landing forces; although the one Indian mountain battery which had landed with the ANZACs had exerted great influence, both by damaging the Turks and by raising Australasian morale by their presence. Efforts were made to improve the bridgeheads, most urgently at 'V' Beach where the landing-forces still held little more than the shoreline. On 26 April Sedd-el-Bahr was captured, and as the Turks withdrew the four landing-beaches were linked, the line now encompassing the tip of the peninsula. Two days after the first landing, Hamilton was reinforced by the French who had been evacuated from Kum Kale in the face of two Turkish divisions.

The First Battle of Krithia

Hamilton was anxious to occupy the heights of Achi Baba, possession of which would allow his artillery to range over the entire area, and ordered an offensive for 28 April, conducted by Hunter-Weston and known as the First Battle of Krithia.

The new lines established by the Turks in front of Krithia, under Achi Baba, were attacked by 29th Division on the left (87 Brigade left, 88 right, 86 in reserve), and the French 1st Division on the right, with the 2nd South Wales Borderers on the French right. Although by mid-morning the British were actually on the slopes of Achi Baba, the 29th had been so badly mauled in the landings that a spirited Turkish counter-attack drove them off. On this occasion Hamilton intervened in person, sending an aide ashore to stabilize the line; but the difficult terrain and Hunter-Weston's failure to co-ordinate the various elements of his force prevented success and the Allies withdrew, having sustained some 3,000 casualties from the 14,000 engaged.

Although by 28 April the bulk of the British forces were ashore, there was such confusion in the landing of equipment that until this chaos was remedied and the troops rested, no further operations were feasible. Renewed Turkish attacks had been made at Anzac, but the Australasians had interrupted their digging to throw back the Turks, even in hand-to-hand bayonet-fights, and they held on despite heavy casualties (on 26/27 April alone 1st Australian Division had sustained 4,500 casualties, about two-fifths of the division's infantry). Hamilton noted that he was unable to conduct any offensive as half his men spent their time carrying water and supplies from the beaches to where the other half were digging; he was desperately in need of ammunition and reinforcements, but believed that these were not available as Kitchener had made it clear that he already had all the troops that could be spared. Three weeks before the landing, however, Kitchener had

▶ *A wounded Turkish prisoner is assisted by his captor. Note the latter's cap with ear-flaps, and* *shorts probably fabricated by cutting the lower leg off the ordinary trousers.*

▲ *French naval picket-boats (left foreground) tie up to the bridge of boats running from the River Clyde to the shore; British troops go ashore (right). In the background are the ruins of Sedd-el-Bahr fort.*

▶ *A trench of the Turkish 125th Regiment (16th Division); second from the right, wearing a turban, is an Imam or regimental Muslim chaplain. (Australian War Memorial, neg. no. A 2598)*

▲ The heights of Achi Baba: this was the unimposing high ground disputed at such bitter cost throughout the Allies' occupation of Helles. Turkish barbed wire is in the foreground.

◀ Members of the 14th Sikhs in 'Big Gully', Helles.

◀ A French '75' in position at the right of the Allied line at Helles. To the left of the gun is the limber, turned upon its side, allowing access to the ammunition through the open top. Two of the crew wear kepis, but the remainder have the distinctively shaped French topee.

changed his mind and authorized the use of as many men as could be spared from the Egypt garrison, which decision he communicated to the British commandant in Egypt, Sir John Maxwell; but incredibly, no one told Hamilton. As Hamilton had thus not requested troops from Maxwell, it was believed that they were not needed; only after Admirals Guépratte and de Robeck informed the Admiralty of the progress of the expedition did Kitchener appreciate that reinforcements were needed. The 42nd Division and 29 Indian Brigade were ordered to be dispatched from Egypt. Meanwhile, Hamilton dug in, evacuated his 5,000 casualties, and awaited the reinforcements which he eventually realized were at his disposal.

Liman von Sanders spent the respite reorganizing his forces, having begun to transfer his divisions covering Bulair to the battle-front on the evening of the landing. In addition, he brought a division by boat from the Asiatic shore and received two more from Constantinople, swelling his forces to some 75 battalions. Enver Pasha ordered a full-scale attack, and after a bombardment of the whole of the Allied line the major offensive was launched on 1 May, by some 16,000 men with 2,000 in reserve. The attacks were brave but hopeless, and the Turks were driven back; renewed assaults on the succeeding two nights fared no better, but the casualties they inflicted worsened Hamilton's position. The French suffered so severely that the 2 Naval Brigade had to take over part of their line, and on the night of 5/6 May 2 Australian Brigade and the New Zealand Infantry Brigade were shipped from Anzac to Helles; and the leading elements (125 Lancashire Fusilier Brigade) of 42nd Division had disembarked from Egypt.

The Second Battle of Krithia

With these reinforcements, Hamilton planned a new offensive on Achi Baba, the Second Battle of Krithia. He remained off-shore, having transferred his staff to a new command-ship, *Arcadian*. The Allied forces were reorganized for the assault: 125 and 29 Indian Brigades were attached to the ravaged 29th Division, a new division was formed from the two ANZAC and 1 Naval Brigades, and 2

▲ *Lieutenant-colonel, British staff. Many British troops wore a uniform that made little concession to the Dardanelles climate. This figure wears the ordinary service uniform, with rank-badges upon the shoulder-straps, less obvious than those worn on the cuffs, worn in tropical uniform and adopted progressively by officers serving in Europe.*

The staff appointment is indicated by the scarlet gorget-patch with crimson braid stripe; hence the nickname 'red tabs' applied to staff officers in general. He wears the ribbon of the Military Cross, a decoration instituted on 28 December 1914 for award to captains, subalterns and warrant officers. (Painting by G. A. Embleton)

ORDER OF BATTLE
Reinforcements prior to Suvla
(principal units only)

42nd (East Lancashire) Division
125 (Lancashire Fusilier) Brigade: 5/, 6/, 7/ and 8/ Lancashire Fusiliers
126 (East Lancashire) Brigade: 4/ and 5/East Lancashire Regiment; 9/ and 10/Manchester Regiment
127 (Manchester) Brigade: 5/, 6/, 7/ and 8/Manchester Regiment

29 Indian Brigade:
1/5th, 1/6th and 2/10th Gurkha Rifles; 14th Prince of Wales's Own Ferozepore Sikhs

52nd Lowland Division
155 (South Scottish) Brigade: 4/ and 5/ Royal Scots Fusiliers; 4/ and 5/King's Own Scottish Borderers
156 (Scottish Rifle) Brigade: 4/ and 7/Royal Scots; 7/ and 8/Cameronians
157 (Highland Light Infantry) Brigade: 5/, 6/ and 7/ Highland Light Infantry; 5/Argyll and Sutherland Highlanders

2nd French Division
3 Metropolitan Brigade: 176th Regiment; 2nd African Regiment
Colonial Brigade: 7th and 8th Colonial Regiments

2 Australian Light Horse Brigade:
5th Queensland; 6th and 7th New South Wales Regiments

3 Australian Light Horse Brigade:
8th Victoria, 9th Victoria and S. Australian, 10th W. Australian Regiments

New Zealand Mounted Brigade:
Auckland, Canterbury, and Wellington Mounted Rifles

Naval Brigade remained attached to the French 1st Division; not until 6–8 May did the French 2nd Division arrive. The ANZAC/Naval division remained as the reserve and was not committed until the second and third days. Little progress was made on 6 May, but following a heavy bombardment by artillery and the fleet, by 8 May between 400 and 600 yards had been gained, but not the high ground, from where the Turks maintained their artillery observation. Their wire and machine-gun post remained a most formidable obstacle. Hamilton wisely suggested that the advance should be made at night; Hunter-Weston disagreed and so the attacks went in during daylight, and were predictably slaughtered. Having failed once, Hunter-Weston could do no more than repeat the tactic; consequently, when the offensive was called off after 8 May, the Allies had sustained 6,500 casualties. (The splendid Australians had been severely hit: their 2 Brigade suffered 1,056 casualties out of 2,900, and the 6th (Victoria) Battalion had only one officer left, but as usual on such occasions NCOs or even enlisted men took command and carried on.)

With the situation stalemated, Hamilton requested further divisions from Kitchener; but Keyes, convinced that the great Allied fleet could force the Narrows, persuaded de Robeck to call a council of war to discuss a renewed naval attempt to batter through to the Sea of Marmara. A somewhat unenthusiastic message was cabled to London that the admirals were prepared to try again. Opinion in London was divided; Italy had recently entered the war and had asked for British naval support, necessitating some diminution in de Robeck's fleet. Churchill was anxious to pursue the Dardanelles venture, but was unwilling to damage Anglo-Italian relations; Fisher was now ardently against the entire scheme. Whatever chance there might have been for a resumption of the naval attack disappeared when the old battleship *Goliath* was torpedoed and sunk on 12 May in the Dardanelles; consequently, de Robeck was ordered not to renew the attack but to send *Queen Elizabeth* home to safety. Fisher resigned over the dispatch of further ships to the Dardanelles, and the growing political crisis compelled Asquith to form a coalition government. Churchill, seen as the author of the scheme even though the blame for its mishandling was not his, was removed from the Admiralty, but was given a seat in the newly formed Dardanelles Committee, established specifically to conduct the campaign.

All now depended upon Hamilton, whose original plan to drive up from Helles now seemed to alter to consolidation at the toe of the peninsula (capturing Achi Baba to make the beaches more secure), and mounting the main offensive from Anzac. Hamilton was being badgered by Kitchener and was receiving reports of considerable Turkish reinforcements, but his position was strengthening: among new arrivals at Anzac were the

Australian Light Horse and New Zealand Mounted Rifles, among the best troops in the army.

Turkish Counter-Attack at Anzac

Before Hamilton initiated the Third Battle of Krithia, the Turks launched a major attack upon Anzac. The opposing trenches were within hailing distance, sometimes no more than five yards apart, in which conditions even a small rise or defensive gully attained great tactical significance. In the usual way, trenches and features of terrain were given homely names, often of the home-towns of those who first occupied them, or from officers who had distinguished themselves. Thus, at Anzac, the front line ran along Walker's Ridge, Russell's Top, Quinn's Post, Courtney's Post; with routes to the front line via Monash Gully, Shrapnel Gully, Victoria Gully, and the areas under enemy control included Lone Pine (from a tree) and Johnston's Jolly, from Brigadier-General G.J. Johnston, commanding 2nd Australian Division's artillery, who directed their fire to 'jolly up' the Turks! Along these positions the ANZACs existed in a barren, inhospitable landscape, short of water, beset by flies (one of the most enduring memories of Gallipoli), in the burning heat, and unable to relax except in the rare periods of relief on the beaches, when even bathing or games of cricket were always likely to be under fire.

Snipers were ever active on both sides; on 15 May General Sir William Bridges, commanding 1st Australian Division, was killed by a sniper in Monash Gully. The Allies' weapons were not ideal for this type of warfare: compounding the constant lack of heavy artillery and usual shortage of ammunition, trench-mortars were in very short supply, as they had not been thought necessary, and no provision at all had been made for hand-

▶ *Top: An Australian trench at Walker's Ridge in May 1915. The man holding the rifle is believed to have been the father of the soldier in the foreground. (Australian War Memorial, neg. no. C 667)*

▶ *Australians with a captured Turkish sniper, camouflaged with foliage. The regulation uniform degenerated progressively to shirt-sleeves and shorts, until the ANZACs were described as 'the naked Australians'.*

◀ Manufacturing hand-grenades: empty tin cans are converted to 'jam tin bombs'. The man at extreme right is using an anvil upon which to cut up lengths of barbed wire to pack into the tins to act as shrapnel.

▼ Cricket on Shell Green, Anzac. Not even the threat of Turkish fire was sufficient to discourage Australia's national game; indeed, the cricketing prowess of Lieutenant Massie (known in 1 Australian Brigade as 'Massive') was such that it was noted he could throw a grenade farther than any man on Gallipoli! (Australian War Memorial, neg. no. G 1289)

grenades. Large numbers of spherical grenades (nicknamed 'cricket balls' by the British and ANZACs) were employed by the Turks, to reply to which large numbers of grenades were manufactured from tin cans by the British and Australians. Colloquially styled 'jam-tin bombs', these home-made weapons comprised bursting-charges and lumps of scrap metal (even bits of barbed wire) packed into used tin cans.

Despite the terrible conditions, the spirit of the ANZACs was such that they held on, against desperate and heroic Turkish assaults. One such attack was made by up to 30,000 Turks on 19 May, a succession of massed charges in dense formation, pressed home with suicidal bravery along the centre of the ANZAC position. (Liman von Sanders claimed the responsibility for the attack, but it is possible that it was instigated by Enver.) Having suffered 10,000 casualties (to the ANZACs' 100 dead and 500 wounded), the Turks abandoned the attack. An attack on the night of 19/20 May actually captured the forward trench at Courtney's Post, but the Turks were evicted by

◄ *Major, 2nd Mounted Division. This staff officer wears a typical service uniform modified for hot climates: the tunic bears the rank-insignia on the cuffs and the red gorget-patches of staff appointment, with the topee issued to some units for the Dardanelles campaign. The brassard or 'armlet' was worn by staff officers, sometimes bearing a formation-badge, but in this case lettered with the identity of the division. The pennant in the background is that of the 29th Division. (Painting by Mike Chappell)*

▲ *British infantry in tropical uniform. A popular style for service in hot climates was shirt, shorts and topee, the latter sometimes bearing regimental insignia. The equipment illustrated here is the so-called 1914 pattern, produced in leather as an emergency measure to compensate for a shortage of the regulation 1908-pattern webbing equipment. (Painting by Mike Chappell)*

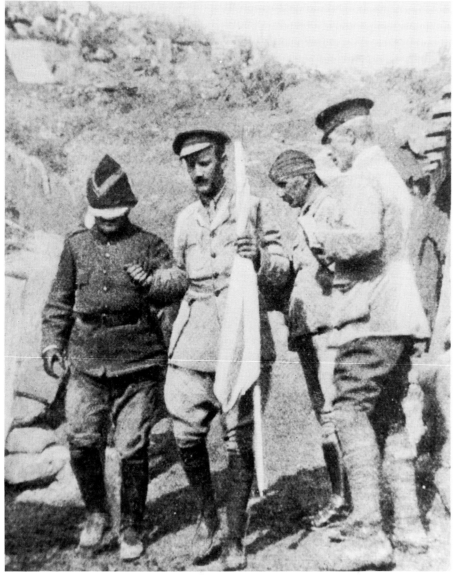

▲ One of the commonest sights on the peninsula: dead Turks at Anzac. These men had been killed on 19 May; the photograph was taken during the armistice on 24 May, when a temporary cessation of hostilities had to be arranged to dispose of thousands of decomposing bodies, which provided an intolerable hazard to the health of both sides. The men standing in the background are ANZACs. (Australian War Memorial, neg. no. G 1440A)

◄ Negotiating for the truce at Anzac to allow both sides to bury the dead: a blindfolded Turkish envoy is guided through the ANZAC lines.

► Wounded prisoners were generally well-treated by both sides, despite the savage nature of the fighting during the campaign. Here, an ANZAC gives a wounded Turk a drink. The hill in the background is Achi Baba; the terrain is typical of the scrub that covered much of the Gallipoli peninsula. (Australian War Memorial, neg. no. G 271)

Lance-Corporal Albert Jacka of the 14th (Victoria) Battalion, 'greased lightning with the bayonet', who shot five and bayonetted two more. He became the ANZACs' first VC of the war, and probably their most famous. A new hazard to both sides now appeared: the danger of disease from the thousands of unburied bodies putrefying in the extreme heat (not for nothing was the insect-life of Gallipoli referred to as 'corpse-flies'). A truce was agreed between the two armies for 24 May, when the bodies were buried, and its terms of a temporary suspension of hostilities were observed scrupulously, proving to the ANZACs that 'Johnny Turk' or 'Abdul' was not an unprincipled heathen as the propaganda stated, but 'a good clean fighter' as the poet 'Argent' wrote.

The Third Battle of Krithia

At Helles, conditions were little different from those at Anzac. The brigades borrowed from Anzac were returned there shortly before the great Turkish attack, but although reinforcements had swelled the Allied forces, some had begun to despair at the management of the campaign. The Reverend Oswin Creighton, padre to 86 Brigade

and author of *With the 29th Division in Gallipoli* (London 1916), remarked on 18 May that the expedition was 'an utterly fool-hardy and under-estimated enterprise', and that they were so stuck that 'the whole world is in a pretty good muddle'.

Hunter-Weston insisted upon the maintenance of an offensive spirit, the most remarkable example of which was the seizure of a position at the north end of 'Y' Beach by a small detachment of the 1/6th Gurkhas on the night of 12 May, covered by naval gunfire, which gained more than a quarter of a mile at negligible cost. Hunter-Weston appreciated the advantages of nocturnal operations, but does not seem to have considered making a major offensive at night, presumably believing that its hazards outweighed the advantages of surprise and consequent limitations of casualties; instead, he continued to have his command slaughtered by unimaginative attacks in daylight. On 24 May Hunter-Weston was promoted to Lieutenant-General and given command of the newly designated VIII Corps, comprising all the British forces at Helles; following d'Amade's recall, the French were now led by General Henri Gouraud. The French made some progress against the Turkish positions in their front (despite a costly and unsuccessful attempt to capture the strongpoint they had named 'Haricot' on 21 June), but they remained exposed to fire in their rear from Turkish positions on the Asiatic Coast.

The next major attempt to take Achi Baba was the Third Battle of Krithia which began on 4 June, planned largely by Hunter-Weston and Gouraud and involving (from right to left) the 1st French and 2nd French Divisions, 2 Naval Brigade, and 42nd and 29th Divisions. To supplement the British artillery (still suffering from shortages of shells), they were lent six batteries of the superb French 75mm guns. Some 30,000 men were employed in the operation, two-thirds in the initial assault; but they were opposed by between 25,000 and 28,000 Turks, well-established in prepared positions, with 86 pieces of artillery, and with morale not as damaged by their recent appalling losses at Anzac as the Allied commanders suspected. Advancing yet again in broad daylight (the preliminary bombardment began at 8 a.m., with the assault commencing at noon), the Allies made some progress, but a spirited counter-attack drove the French from the trenches they had gained. In such an attack on a broad front, one reverse could undo the whole operation, and the re-occupation of the ground initially captured by the French allowed the Turks to enfilade, the right flank of 2 Naval Brigade, which fell back with immense loss. The 42nd Division had made considerable gains, but the withdrawal of the Naval Brigade exposed their flank, and they had to retire in the evening, followed by 29th Division. The British alone lost 4,000 casulaties in this costly failure, and its success at some points so alarmed the Turks that they began extending their trench-system, making it even more formidable.

In early June the Allies at Helles were strengthened further by the arrival of the 52nd (Lowland) Division; but this could not compensate for the troops lost in the succession of ill-conceived operations. Padre Creighton observed on 8 June that of the 2nd Royal Fusiliers of 86 Brigade, only one officer was left (they had lost the ten replacement officers who had joined since landing); but, he remarked, some were even worse hit: when the 2nd Hampshire Regiment was given a respite from the front line, only 100-odd men were left, and not one officer. Losses in the Turkish divisions were in general even more severe.

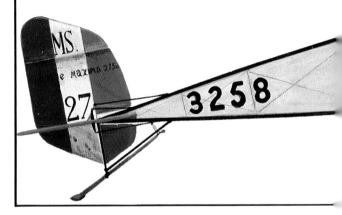

▼ *Morane Saulnier Type L. No. 3258 was one of six Royal Naval Air Service Type L Moranes shipped to the Aegean, where they formed part of the equipment of No. 3 Wing RNAS at Mudros in August 1915. The French-designed monoplanes were not popular with the naval airmen and were soon replaced by Voisin biplanes. 3258 is shown fitted with a primitive rack between the under-carriage legs, which normally carried up to six 201b Hales bombs. (Painting by Ray Rimell)*

◀ *British artillery in action, with gunners fuzing shells in the foreground. The gun bears the chalked name 'Annie', a somewhat ironic christening, as 'Asiatic Annie' was a Turkish gun which shelled Allied rear areas from the Asiatic shore.*

▶ *Quinn's Post, Anzac, during the attack of 28 May, the day on which Major H. Quinn of the 15th (Queensland & Tasmania) Battalion was killed, from whom the location took its name. Behind the sandbags in the left midground is a sniper, his observer looking through binoculars. (Australian War Memorial, neg. no. G 1006)*

STALEMATE

During the period of the Battles of Krithia, Allied submarines had caused considerable havoc by slipping into the Sea of Marmara: panic was caused in Constantinople by the depredations of the British Lieutenant-Commander Martin Nasmith in the submarine *E 11*, who was awarded the Victoria Cross for taking the war right up to the Turkish capital. An equally important submarine operation was that carried out by Lieutenant-Commander Otto Hersing, who had sailed the *U 21* from Germany, through the Mediterranean. On the morning of 25 May, when Nasmith was torpedoing a Turkish freighter berthed at Constantinople itself, *U 21* torpedoed the British battleship *Triumph* off Gaba Tepe. De Robeck at once ordered all his capital ships to withdraw to the safety of Mudros harbour, save for the old battleship *Majestic*, which remained with the destroyers off Helles, until she too was sunk by *U 21*. The departure of *Queen Elizabeth* had already dented British morale, and this was compounded by the withdrawal of the other capital ships; but the cruise of *E 11* and similar submarines redressed the balance. Henceforth, large-scale reinforcement of Liman von Sanders by sea was impossible because of the danger of submarine attack. Although small vessels carried supplies by night, most had now to make a rail journey of 150 miles, followed by five days' march, before reaching their destination. Liman von Sanders admitted that had the coastal route been severed completely, the Fifth Army would have been unable to sustain its operations for want of supplies. The effect on Turkish morale, especially Nasmith's raid on Constantinople, demonstrated what would have occurred had the entire fleet been able to penetrate the Narrows. Although eight Allied submarines were lost, the damage they had caused, especially to Turkish morale, was immense: Nasmith sank the battleship *Häirredin Barbarousse*

in August, shelled the coast, and even landed a saboteur to blow up a bridge. In this respect at least, the operations in the Dardanelles area were conspicuously successful.

On 7 June the Dardanelles Committee assembled to review two proposals, both committed to holding the position on the Gallipoli peninsula, but while Kitchener wanted Hamilton to progress slowly, Churchill suggested a major reinforcement. The latter was accepted by Kitchener, and Hamilton was informed that three 'New Army' divisions would be put at his disposal. Gouraud urged that these be landed either north of Bulair, or on the Adriatic coast to attack Chanak. On 30 June, however, the gallant Gouraud was severely injured (losing an arm) crossing 'V' Beach to visit hospitalized French soldiers, and command passed to General Maurice Bailloud, commander of the French 2nd Division. He pressed for the Asiatic landing but Hamilton declined, thinking that in the present circumstances his forces were already sufficiently divided, between Helles and Anzac.

Following the failure of the great Turkish attack on Anzac, operations in that sector became considerably quieter. Skirmishes occurred constantly around strongpoints like Pope's Hill and Quinn's Post (both guarding the head of Monash Gully), where fighting remained extremely bitter. Although the Turks were short of ammunition, they still enjoyed an advantage in artillery over the ANZACs, whose cramped bridgehead and the nature of the terrain limited their scope for deployment of guns; and since the withdrawal of the capital ships in the face of the U-boat threat, heavy naval gunfire was no longer available. The Australasians continued to toil, building dugouts, trenches and pathways, and landing supplies, the latter difficult from the limited space and often unfavourable sea conditions. Although condensing plant and reservoirs were established, there was

▶ *HMS* Triumph, *sunk by U 21 on 25 May.*

▶ *HMS* Majestic, *the last of the Allied capital ships to remain on station off Helles, sunk by U 21 on 27 May.*

▶ *The British E 7, one of a number of Allied submarines which caused havoc in the Sea of Marmara, having secretly slipped through the Narrows. E 7 was destroyed on 5 September after becoming entangled in an anti-submarine net.*

still a water shortage, and the entire area was under threat from Turkish artillery at every moment. Under these terrible conditions the ANZACs were transformed from amateurs into a battle-hardened force.

The lull in serious fighting was used by the Turks to strengthen their positions, so that an extensive system of trenches guarded against a breakthrough from Anzac towards Boghali; the ridges descending from Sari Bair (naturally strong positions) were fortified further, the area around Lone Pine being made into a particularly tough strongpoint. The scrub-covered terrain was such that even British aerial reconnaissance could provide no clear picture of battery-positions upon which the ANZAC artillery could range.

◀ *A Turkish trench and dug-out, camouflaged against Allied aerial observation.*

◀ *The terrain was in many places so difficult that the only method of transporting supplies was by human muscle. This party of ANZACs is festooned with shells, to be manhandled laboriously to the artillery batteries at the front. They wear typical Gallipoli uniform, shirt or vest and shorts, with a mixture of head-dress. (Australian War Memorial, neg. no. C 3374)*

In addition to the continual minor raiding, sniping and bombardment at Anzac, two larger actions were fought. On 28 June the ANZACs mounted a demonstration at the extreme right of their position, from Tasman Post towards Pine Ridge, to occupy Turkish attention and prevent them from transferring resources to oppose the attack at Helles (for which see below); when the Turks responded their supporting columns came under fire from both the ANZAC artillery and British destroyers. In retaliation, the Turks mounted a counter-attack upon the Quinn's Post – Pope's Hill sector on the night of 29/30 June; fighting continued until daylight and cost the Turks so heavily that they launched no further offensives.

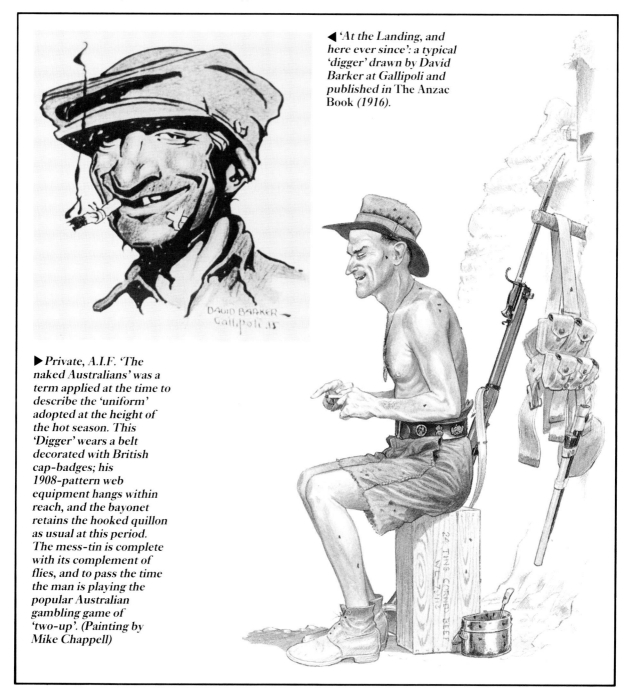

◀ 'At the Landing, and here ever since': a typical 'digger' drawn by David Barker at Gallipoli and published in The Anzac Book (1916).

▶ Private, A.I.F. 'The naked Australians' was a term applied at the time to describe the 'uniform' adopted at the height of the hot season. This 'Digger' wears a belt decorated with British cap-badges; his 1908-pattern web equipment hangs within reach, and the bayonet retains the hooked quillon as usual at this period. The mess-tin is complete with its complement of flies, and to pass the time the man is playing the popular Australian gambling game of 'two-up'. (Painting by Mike Chappell)

▲ Officers of the 2nd Royal Fusiliers in a trench at Helles: standing right is Lieutenant Lionel Clement Mundy, acting ad- jutant, who was killed on 6 June. His companion was the last of the battalion's officers to remain unscathed.

▲ Sniping with a periscope-rifle. This device, invented by Lance-Corporal W. C. Beech of the 2nd (New South Wales) Battalion, allowed sniping to be conducted with accuracy without the sniper having to show himself. This sniper is accompanied by an observer using an ordinary periscope.

Prior to the arrival of the major reinforcement, the main actions were in the Helles sector. On 21 June, the two French divisions captured some trenches on the right of the line, and on the other flank an attack by 29th and 52nd Divisions on 28 June pushed the Allied line from Gurkha Bluff to Fusilier Bluff, taking as a result several hundred yards of Gully Ravine. It was remarked that part of the success of this operation was due to the loan to the British of two French mortars which dropped bombs vertically into the Turkish trenches. The only examples of this valuable weapon available to the entire British force at this time were six Japanese weapons, with inadequate ammunition. (It should be remarked here that preliminary bombardments had to be carried out almost entirely by field-guns; unlike operations on the Western Front, the participation of howitzers and heavier ordnance was very limited. Although the British eventually possessed some field howitzers and a few 60pdrs, there were great difficulties in landing them, and ammunition was always limited. The French had no howitzers but a more plentiful supply of rounds.)

Despite the ground gained, it is arguable that it warranted the 3,800 casualties. Turkish counter-attacks on the succeeding two nights were repelled, and cost them some 16,000 men. On 12/13 July Hunter-Weston made another attack on a mile-wide front by 52nd Division, which succeeded in occupying some of the Turkish front-line trenches, but at a cost of 4,000 casualties (against about 10,000 Turkish). Despite heavy losses on the first day, Hunter-Weston bludgeoned forward again next day, with the same depressing results, the already partially exhausted Royal Naval Division suffering severely. Indeed, Major-General G. G. A. Egerton, commanding 52nd Division, described the operation as a wicked and useless slaughter of his command, and despite the ground won, the Turks still held Achi Baba. Even the immense Turkish casualties were not a major setback for them, for now reinforcements were being fed in from the Turkish Second Army. On 20 July Hunter-Weston fell ill and was invalided home. His exit was probably not lamented by the units that had endured the butchery of his uninspired frontal assaults.

SARI BAIR

It having been determined that the only chance of success was a major offensive, Hamilton was allocated five new divisions: the 10th, 11th and 13th, which together formed a new IX Corps, with 53rd and 54th Divisions attached. Hamilton requested a capable and experienced officer to command it, either Generals Byng or Rawlinson, then occupied on the Western Front. As both of these were junior to Lieutenant-General Sir Bryan Mahon, commander of the 10th Division, Kitchener chose instead Lieutenant-General Sir Frederick Stopford, elderly, somewhat infirm, and who had never commanded a large formation. A worse choice could hardly have been made.

Conditions on the peninsula were bad, the troops worn down by constant exposure to danger; as Chaplain Creighton wrote, 'You cannot rest a regiment without a few men getting hit every day . . . It is a wonder to me how calmly everyone takes the situation . . . Do people realize our conditions. I wonder, in England? I don't quite see why we should be the only people who do . . .' Rations remained rudimentary, and almost all water had to be brought from Egypt: there were no wells at Helles, and only a couple of springs; at Anzac the shortage was even worse despite the condensing-plant producing drinking-water from the sea. At times men were reduced to less than three pints per day for all purposes; this in an area where for sixteen hours a day the sun beat down so unmercifully that uncovered rations melted in their tin containers. (Conversely, while the Turkish army was customarily short of almost everything, they had an abundance of water from the springs in the high ground which they held.)

Over the whole area was the stench of putrefying corpses, upon which the plague of flies existed; and from June virtually the entire army was affected by dysentery, which in many cases proved fatal. It had been intended to establish hospitals on the peninsula, but so little ground had been won that this was not possible. The main tented hospital was established on the island of Lemnos, from where a constant shuttle of hospital-ships took the more severely wounded to Egypt, Malta or Britain. Such were the demands placed on the medical services that they could hardly cope. From the beginning of June Hamilton's headquarters was on the island of Imbros, where he was sufficiently distant to be shielded from the full horror of existence on the peninsula.

A New Landing: Suvla Bay

With his reinforcement, Hamilton would have at his disposal some 120,000 men (considerably less

▲ *For all ranks, existence at Gallipoli was equally arduous: this sandbagged and tented hole was the headquarters of the* Australian 4 Brigade, below Sari Bair. (Australian War Memorial, neg. no. A 2026)

◀ *Casualty-evacuation at Anzac: some terrain was so rough that it was impossible for stretchers to be carried. Despite carrying his mate, this 'digger' retains his rifle and fixed bayonet. (Australian War Memorial, neg. no. G 599)*

than the establishment of thirteen divisions). The new troops, however, were not of the quality of those who had landed in April, but were completely raw: the 10th, 11th and 13th Divisions were 'New Army' and contained hardly any experienced personnel, and the 53rd and 54th were Territorials. This was especially fatal considering the incompetence of the leadership.

Churchill favoured landing these new formations on the Bulair isthmus, but this was rejected, partly because de Robeck thought the submarine danger in the Gulf of Saros was too great. Hamilton decided to develop the bridgehead at Anzac, but because the ground already held was so cramped, the new corps was ordered to land at Suvla Bay, five miles north of Anzac Cove. This area was known to be only lightly defended, and only four miles of open ground needed to be crossed before the high ground could be occupied: Kiritch Tepe to the north, Tekke Tepe to the north-east of Suvla Bay, and the Anafarta Spur to the east. The Turkish right flank could thus be turned and a breakout from Anzac could occupy the Sari Bair ridge with its high point of Koja Chemen Tepe, alias Hill 971, the key to the area, the Narrows and thus to the entire campaign. A successful landing at Suvla could thus achieve in one determined advance what several months of campaigning had failed to accomplish. To assist

the landing, Hamilton had at his disposal purpose-built, armoured landing-craft or 'beetles', increased aerial observation (balloon-ships and carrier-borne seaplanes) and, to replace the fire-power of the withdrawn battleships, 'monitors', flat-bottomed ships armed with 14in guns and with 'blisters' on the sides to minimize the effect of torpedo-strikes. Three old cruisers were similarly equipped: *Endymion*, *Talbot* and *Theseus*. Although Hamilton's field artillery was reasonably strong (by the end of July there were 124 guns at Helles, rather more than half that number at Anzac), the heavier guns and field howitzers needed to make a real impression on the Turkish defence-works were still lacking. (A howitzer brigade was dispatched belatedly to the Dardanelles at the end of July, but it did not arrive in time to assist the opening of the attack).

At the time of the initial landing, Liman von Sanders had to cover a number of possible locations for the renewal of the Allied offensive. In early August he maintained three divisions on the Asiatic coast at Kum Kale; the peninsula was divided into northern and southern zones by a line just south of Gaba Tepe and Maidos, and included three main forces. Three divisions were at Bulair, commanded by Feizi Bey, covering the north; three divisions at Anzac, commanded by Essad Pasha, five on the Helles front, commanded by

Wehib Pasha (Essad's brother), and two south of Gaba Tepe forming a link between the forces at Helles and Anzac. Suvla was covered by a small force styled the Anafarta Detachment, of which more below. Mustafa Kemal's position was difficult at this period. Liman von Sanders respected his military ability, but was unable to promote him for political reasons. Kemal resigned twice over the interference of and criticism by Enver Pasha during one of the latter's periodic visits to the front, and not until Enver had departed was Kemal persuaded to resume command of his 19th Division on the Anzac front. Even the position of Liman von Sanders himself was not secure: being perceived as having no idea save dig in and defend, the German high command ordered him on 26 July to turn his command over to Field Marshal von der Goltz and return to Germany to report. He managed to avoid taking this drastic step, and the great Allied attack prevented any further change of command, though Liman von Sanders was forced to accept the 'assistance' of an aide, Colonel von Lossow, appointed to oversee his actions.

Diversionary Attacks

Hamilton scheduled the Suvla landing for 6 August, and ordered two simultaneous diversionary attacks to occupy the Turks, at Helles and Anzac. The offensive at Helles can be covered briefly. On the afternoon of 6 August the main attack fell upon a 1,200-yard front of the heavily fortified centre of the Turkish position. Instead of a demonstration, it was unwisely turned into an attempt to capture Krithia and Achi Baba again; what ground was gained was recovered by a Turkish counter-attack, followed by a heavier attack on the night of 12/13 August, but they were themselves counter-attacked by the British next day and the position stabilized. The British attack had been very wasteful, and far from drawing additional Turkish forces into the southern zone, it did not prevent the transfer of the Turkish 4th Division to the vicinity of Anzac, but was at least sufficient to prevent a more wholesale transfer to the northern zone.

The operation from Anzac was an entirely different case. To the forces already at Anzac, Hamilton added 13th Division, which with 29 Indian Brigade gave Birdwood some 40,000 men. The reinforcement was slipped ashore at night on 4–6 August and the troops secreted in newly constructed trenches and caves, to conceal their arrival from the Turks. The plan was for an attack at Lone Pine, to the south of the ANZAC bridgehead, utilizing a secretly constructed underground tunnel which would allow the assaulting force to debouch almost directly into the Turkish positions. Having convinced the Turks that this was the main attack, after dark the principal assault would be made further north, towards Sari Bair, which was hoped to be in ANZAC hands by the following morning.

On the afternoon of 6 August the assault was delivered at Lone Pine. The area from Russell's

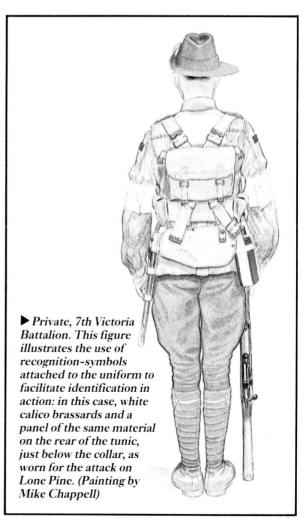

▶ *Private, 7th Victoria Battalion. This figure illustrates the use of recognition-symbols attached to the uniform to facilitate identification in action: in this case, white calico brassards and a panel of the same material on the rear of the tunic, just below the collar, as worn for the attack on Lone Pine. (Painting by Mike Chappell)*

Top to the sea at the south of the bridgehead was held by 1st Australian Division and 1 and 3 Light Horse Brigades; the attack on Lone Pine was delivered by 1 Australian Brigade, reinforced by the 7th and 12th Battalions from 2 and 3 Brigades respectively. It was a truly desperate assault, made along a front of only some 220 yards, against strongly built trenches roofed over to form strongpoints. Much of the fighting was literally hand-to-hand and extremely confused; it lasted until the last of several Turkish counter-attacks on 9 August, but from the evening of 6 August Lone Pine was in Australian hands. Seven Victoria Crosses were won in this action; 1 Australian Brigade sustained more than 1,700 casualties out of 2,900, the 2nd Battalion suffering a casualty-rate of some 74 per cent, yet they clung on to the position. Other efforts were also made on different sections of the Anzac front, most notably the charge of 3 Light Horse Brigade on the morning of 7 August at Russell's Top, north and uphill from Lone Pine. In a campaign marked for mismanagement and bravery, the operation perhaps stands at the head of both categories: against positions of immense strength and in numbers hopelessly insufficient for the task, the light

▲Australian infantry awaiting the attack at Lone Pine. The difficult and inhospitable nature of *the terrain is illustrated graphically. (Australian War Memorial, neg. no. A 847)*

horsemen charged in repeated waves, and were massacred. Their heroism is unimaginable; equally so the orders which threw in wave after wave in a task which was literally suicidal. Almost three-quarters of the brigade's 600 men fell in fifteen minutes.

The Sari Bair Breakout Attempt

As soon as the operation had commenced at Lone Pine, two columns under the direction of General Sir Alexander Godley began their advance upon the Sari Bair range, the right column under Brigadier-General F. E. Johnston, the left under Major-General H. V. Cox of 29 Indian Brigade. It was a task of immense difficulty, the advance conducted largely at night over mountainous terrain which would have been difficult to traverse in daylight and without opposition. Neither column, striking north and east from Anzac, could keep its schedule; the left column halted when Brigadier-General John Monash of 4 Australian

Brigade convinced Cox that his men were exhausted. The right column pressed on and began to establish itself on Rhododendron Spur (named from the oleanders which grew there), a lower prominence west of the high points of the Sari Bair ridge, which were, north-east from Rhododendron Spur and rising in height: Chunuk Bair, Hill Q, and Koja Chemen Tepe.

In the early morning of 7 August, Mustafa Kemal realized that a major offensive was taking place and sent his 19th Division to occupy the main Sari Bair ridge, while Essad Pasha sent Colonel Kannengiesser (of 9th Division, which had been watching the coast south of Gaba Tepe in case of a landing there) with two regiments to the same area. Liman von Sanders at the same time instructed Feizi Bey at Bulair to send a reinforcement south with all possible speed. Until they arrived, the area was open to conquest; but Johnston of the right column halted his men, and by the time Godley insisted he push on, Turkish reinforcements halted any further progress. Godley called off the attack until the following day.

On 8 August both columns were ordered to advance, Cox to take Hill Q and Koja Chemen Tepe, and Johnston Chunuk Bair. Cox divided his thirteen battalions into four columns, but none advanced far enough to support the 1/6th Gurkhas (29 Indian Brigade) which had advanced alone. Devoid of support, Major C. J. L. Allanson of the 1/6th decided to attempt Hill Q on his own, and entrenched almost at the crest; but as Godley knew nothing of this success, he called off the attack, leaving Allanson isolated. Meanwhile, Johnston's force pushed towards Chunuk Bair, the summit of which was taken by companies of the Wellington Battalion (NZ Infantry Brigade). From there they could see the waters of the Narrows; the objective seemed within grasp. But Hill Q overlooked Chunuk Bair, and the Turks opened a devastating fire from both sides; the two Wellington companies clung on until they were almost annihilated.

On 9 August Godley again renewed the attack, Johnston's column assaulting Chunuk Bair, Cox's Hill Q, and the ground between by Brigadier-General A. H. Baldwin's 38 Brigade (13th Division), as yet uncommitted. The latter's advance was slowed by inadequate reconnaissance over difficult terrain; Johnston's force met heavy resistance, and Cox's attack was called off when Baldwin failed to appear. Allanson, still largely unsupported, attacked again under cover of a bombardment by naval vessels in the bay and by the lighter land-based artillery. When it ceased the 1/6th Gurkhas stormed the hill and took it in desperate hand-to-hand combat; then a salvo of shells, almost incontrovertibly from the British ships, was dropped among the Gurkhas. Shattered by this catastrophe, they retired to their original positions and, with Allanson wounded in the mêlée, hung on under command of their medical officer, repelling five Turkish charges which reached within fifteen yards of their position. At nightfall on 9 August the battered New Zealanders on Chunuk Bair were relieved by the 6th Loyal North Lancashire and 5th Wiltshire Regiments (38 and 40 Brigades respectively), and on 10 August Kemal launched a counter-attack which re-possessed the position at a cost of some 5,000 Turkish casualties. The desperation of their attack reflected the critical nature of the situation: Chunuk Bair represented a threat to the entire Turkish position. As Ian Hamilton wrote in his final dispatch, the defenders maintained 'the old traditions of their race' and died where they stood, but to no avail. Eventually, only the 1/6th Gurkhas were left on the upper ridge, and with the greatest reluctance they retired six hours after the remnants of the other units.

The 'Anzac breakout' to the Sari Bair ridge was not an impossible operation, but one of extreme difficulty, in which the courage of the troops was frustrated by the ineptitude of the leadership and by the most determined opposition. Total British casualties in the operation from 6 to 10 August reached 12,000; 13th Division alone lost 6,000 out of 10,500 engaged, and the 9th Warwickshire and 9th Worcestershire Regiments of 38 Brigade were reported as having lost every officer. Some territory had been gained, which helped to establish a larger bridgehead in due course, but effectively the attempt on Sari Bair had failed. The ultimate tragedy is the fact that its original purpose, to cover the landings at Suvla, was betrayed by an even greater mishandling of that operation.

SUVLA

Suvla Bay had three beaches nominated as 'A', 'B' and 'C', for the disembarkation of Stopford's IX Corps. 'A' Beach was overlooked by the ridge of Kiritch Tepe and by a lesser prominence, Hill 10; 'B' and 'C' Beaches were overlooked by Chocolate Hill (named from its colour, with Green Hill nearby) and the hill of Lala Baba. Between 'A' Beach and 'B' and 'C' was the Suvla Salt Lake, dry and gleaming white in summer. The beaches were not difficult to negotiate, nor was the position fortified or garrisoned in strength. The only Turkish forces covering the area was the Anafarta Detachment under the Bavarian Major Willmer, disposed as follows: on Kiritch Tepe, two companies of Gallipoli Gendarmerie; on Hill 10, three companies of Broussa Gendarmerie; on Lala Baba one company of the 1/31st Regiment (which had a sentry-post on Nibrunesi Point, the tip of land at the southern end of Suvla Bay); on Chocolate and Green hills, three companies of the same battalion; and the reserve around W Hill and Baka Baba, well to the east of the landing area. In total, Willmer had some 1,500 men with which to oppose Stopford's 25,000.

It was imperative that the landing at Suvla not be regarded as an end in itself, for the hills immediately overlooking the beach had to be secured at the earliest stage; and with so few defenders, it should have presented no insuperable difficulty to a determined commander. Yet everything went awry from the start; the landing arrangements were planned in such detail that the wider aspect was submerged, and in any case Stopford was not the man to undertake such a task. He was not helped by Hamilton, whose orders to Stopford stated that his primary objective was to get the troops ashore, and only then consider advancing on the surrounding hills and in assisting the breakout from Anzac to the south. Given Stopford's incompetence and the misleading nature of these orders, the operation was doomed from the beginning.

The landing began in the late evening of 6 August, when 32 and 33 Brigades (11th Division) landed, as planned, on 'B' Beach, and secured Lala Baba. They could have pressed on to Hill 10, but no one was sure of its location and an advance in the dark was ruled out. 34 Brigade (11th Division) was supposed to land farther north, on 'A' Beach, but exactly as had occurred at Anzac, the wrong beach was selected and most actually landed south of 'A' Beach, along the spit of land which separated the Salt Lake from the sea. 30 and 31 Brigades (10th Division) were intended to land next morning (7 August) on 'A' Beach, so that when ashore they could push on to secure Kiritch Tepe, while 11th Division mounted the southern half of a pincer which would occupy Chocolate and Green Hills and together advance inland towards Tekke Tepe. However, instead of 'A' Beach, some units of 10th Division were landed on a beach to the north of 'A', and most on 'C' Beach, virtually on top of 11th Division, and near chaos ensued. The guiding hand to bring order was absent; Hamilton was on Imbros, awaiting news, and Stopford had not even landed at Suvla in person, but was commanding from the sloop *Jonquil*. After the initial landing got ashore without the loss of a man, a continuous fusillade was directed towards the beaches by Willmer's small force.

Liman von Sanders thought his position desperate; he calculated that no troops could reinforce Willmer for at least 36 hours, and when they did arrive, in particular Feizi Bey's reinforcement from Bulair (7th and 12th Divisions), they would be exhausted after their forced march. Reinforcements to the Suvla/Anzac area from Krithia, and those ordered to cross from the Asiatic shore at Chanak, would be even more delayed. Despite the confusion at Suvla, a resolute British advance

Suvla Bay and the Anzac breakout

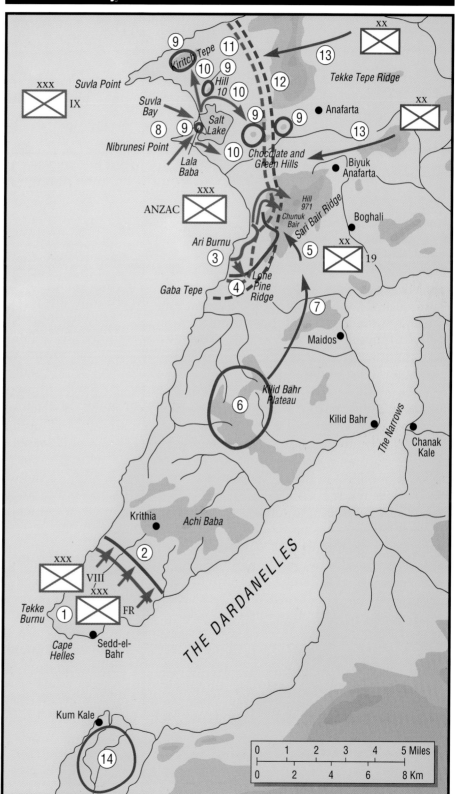

1. Holding attack mounted from Allied lines at Helles, by British VIII Corps (4 divs.) (left and centre of Allied position), and French Corps (2 divs.) (right of Allied position)
2. Turkish forces holding front line at Helles (5 divs.)
3. Breakout from Anzac by ANZAC Corps (3 divs.): feint at Lone Pine, and two attacks north-east upon Sari Bair ridge
4. Turkish front line at Anzac (3 divs.)
5. Counter by Turkish 19th Division against the ANZAC attack on Sari Bair
6. Turkish forces in centre of peninsula (3 divs.)
7. Turkish reinforcement to Anzac front, initially two regiments
8. Landing at Suvla by British IX Corps (3 divs.)
9. Positions of Turkish Anafarta Detachment, initially the only forces available to oppose the Suvla landing
10. British advances from Suvla beach-head
11. (dotted line): ultimate British/ANZAC front line following the joining of the Suvla and Anzac beach-heads
12. (dotted line): ultimate Turkish front line, opposing the Suvla/Anzac position
13. initial Turkish reinforcement from Bulair (7th and 12th Divs., Feizi Bey)
14. Turkish forces holding Asiatic shore, Kum Kale and farther south (3 divs.)

could still have achieved the objective of the landing, but Stopford was anything but resolute, being simply relieved that his troops were ashore and that Hamilton had signalled that he had done 'splendidly'.

As practically nothing had happened at Suvla since the taking of Chocolate Hill at dusk on the 7th – Stopford had still not gone ashore – Hamilton sent an officer to hasten him. This was of no avail, so Hamilton finally went to see for himself. Stopford was still aboard *Jonquil*, resting a strained leg, and declined to accompany Hamilton ashore. Here he found the troops rested but not ready to advance; by the time, upon Hamilton's personal order, that a force had been put together to advance on the surrounding hills, Feizi Bey's exhausted command had arrived and occupied the ridges. The contrast between the actions of the commanders-in-chief was marked: whereas Hamilton only moved when the situation was virtually beyond redemption, Liman von Sanders had been active from the outset and went personally to hasten the arrival of Feizi Bey. When the latter claimed that his exhausted men were unable to attack immediately, Liman von Sanders dismissed him instantly and appointed Mustafa Kemal to overall command. If only Hamilton had been similarly determined, the outcome might have been different; but his character was not sufficiently ruthless to dismiss incompetent subordinates on the spot. As Kannengiesser wrote later, the door to victory was held wide open for Stopford, but he had declined to enter; by the time Hamilton eventually intervened, it was far too late.

A general attack was ordered for 9 August, by which time the Turkish reinforcements were largely in position. The advance was conducted by 11th Division, plus 31 Brigade (10th Division), and the forward elements of 53rd (Welsh) Division which was landing in support. By the time the leading battalion of 32 Brigade (actually the 6th East Yorkshire Regiment, the divisional pioneer battalion) reached the crest of the objective ridge, it found the Turkish reinforcements in position; as the *Official History* was to note, despite the unpardonable delay of two days since the landing, the race for Tekke Tepe was lost by less than thirty minutes. The 10th Division's attempt on Kiritch

ORDER OF BATTLE
The Landing at Suvla, 6/7 August 1915 (principal units only)

10th (Irish) Division
29 Brigade: 10/Hampshire Regiment; 6/Royal Irish Rifles; 5/Connaught Rangers; 6/Leinster Regiment
30 Brigade: 6/ and 7/Royal Munster Fusiliers; 6/ and 7/Royal Dublin Fusiliers
31 Brigade: 5/ and 6/Royal Inniskilling Fusiliers; 5/ and 6/Royal Irish Fusiliers
Pioneer Battalion: 5/Royal Irish Regiment

11th (Northern) Division
32 Brigade: 9/West Yorkshire Regiment; 6/Green Howards; 8/Duke of Wellington's Regiment; 6/York and Lancaster Regiment
33 Brigade: 6/Lincolnshire Regiment; 6/Border Regiment; 7/South Staffordshire Regiment; 9/Sherwood Foresters
34 Brigade: 8/Northumberland Fusiliers; 9/Lancashire Fusiliers; 5/Dorsetshire Regiment; 11/Manchester Regiment
Pioneer Battalion: 6/East Yorkshire Regiment

13th (Western) Division
38 Brigade: 6/King's Own Regiment; 6/East Lancashire Regiment; 6/South Lancashire Regiment; 6/Loyal North Lancashire Regiment
39 Brigade: 9/Royal Warwickshire Regiment; 7/Gloucestershire Regiment; 9/Worcestershire Regiment; 7/North Staffordshire Regiment
40 Brigade: 8/Cheshire Regiment; 8/Royal Welsh Fusiliers; 4/South Wales Borderers; 5/Wiltshire Regiment
Pioneer Battalion: 8/Welsh Regiment

53rd (Welsh) Division
158 (North Wales) Brigade: 5/, 6/ and 7/Royal Welsh Fusiliers; 1/Hereford Regiment
159 (Cheshire) Brigade: 4/ and 7/Cheshire Regiment; 4/ and 5/Welsh Regiment
160 (Welsh Border) Brigade: 2/4th Queen's Regiment; 4/Royal Sussex Regiment; 2/4th Royal West Kent Regiment; 2/10th Middlesex Regiment

54th (East Anglian) Division
161 (Essex) Brigade: 4/, 5/, 6/ and 7/Essex Regiment
162 (East Midland) Brigade: 5/Bedfordshire Regiment; 4/Northamptonshire Regiment; 10/ and 11/London Regiment
163 (Norfolk & Suffolk) Brigade: 4/ and 5/Norfolk Regiment; 5/Suffolk Regiment; 8/Hampshire Regiment

▲British troops advance in waves across the Salt Lake towards the Turkish positions, showing the extremely open ground at Suvla. Smoke from bursting shells is visible in the background.

▶Suvla: a print of a watercolour by Norman Wilkinson showing the view from Chocolate Hill over the bay and to the island of Samothrace in the background. At the left is Lala Baba hill, and in mid-ground the dry Salt Lake. On this print a Suvla veteran has marked in crayon the route of his personal attack on Chocolate Hill, demonstrating the extremely exposed nature of such an advance.

▶Piers and landing-stages built at Suvla.

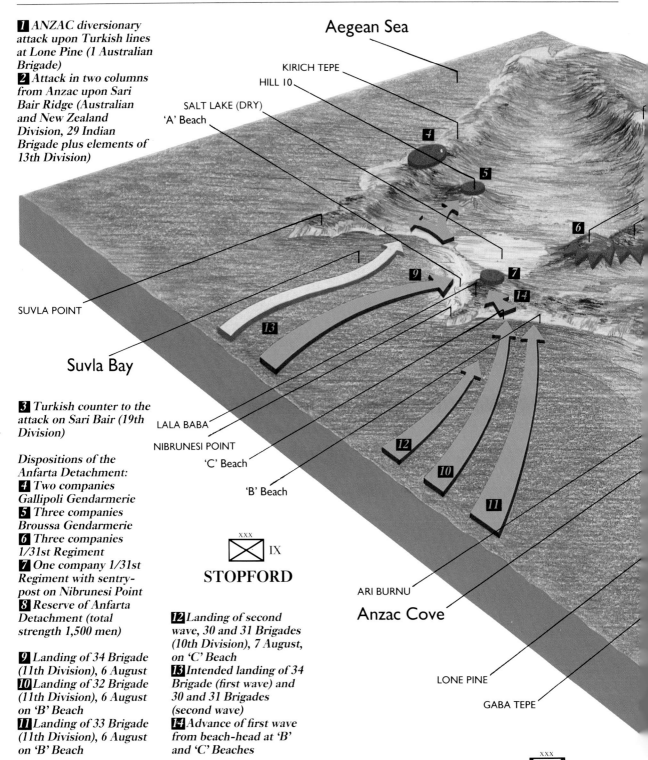

1 *ANZAC diversionary attack upon Turkish lines at Lone Pine (1 Australian Brigade)*
2 *Attack in two columns from Anzac upon Sari Bair Ridge (Australian and New Zealand Division, 29 Indian Brigade plus elements of 13th Division)*

Aegean Sea

KIRICH TEPE
HILL 10
SALT LAKE (DRY)
'A' Beach

SUVLA POINT

Suvla Bay

3 *Turkish counter to the attack on Sari Bair (19th Division)*

LALA BABA
NIBRUNESI POINT
'C' Beach
'B' Beach

Dispositions of the Anfarta Detachment:
4 *Two companies Gallipoli Gendarmerie*
5 *Three companies Broussa Gendarmerie*
6 *Three companies 1/31st Regiment*
7 *One company 1/31st Regiment with sentry-post on Nibrunesi Point*
8 *Reserve of Anfarta Detachment (total strength 1,500 men)*

9 *Landing of 34 Brigade (11th Division), 6 August*
10 *Landing of 32 Brigade (11th Division), 6 August on 'B' Beach*
11 *Landing of 33 Brigade (11th Division), 6 August on 'B' Beach*

xxx
IX
STOPFORD

12 *Landing of second wave, 30 and 31 Brigades (10th Division), 7 August, on 'C' Beach*
13 *Intended landing of 34 Brigade (first wave) and 30 and 31 Brigades (second wave)*
14 *Advance of first wave from beach-head at 'B' and 'C' Beaches*

ARI BURNU

Anzac Cove

LONE PINE
GABA TEPE

xxx ANZAC
BIRDWOOD

SUVLA BAY AND 'ANZAC'

Operations of 6/7 August 1915: the Suvla landing and the Anzac breakout attempt

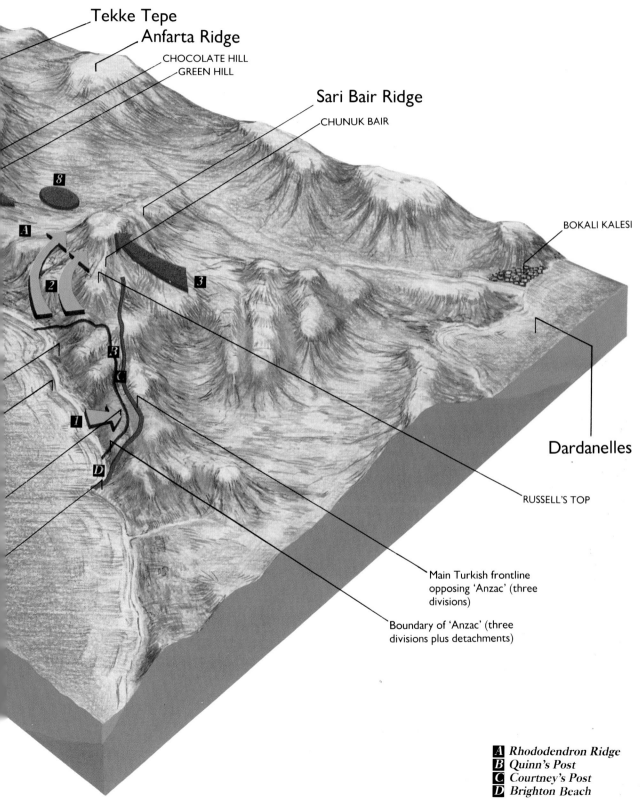

Tekke Tepe

Anfarta Ridge

CHOCOLATE HILL

GREEN HILL

Sari Bair Ridge

CHUNUK BAIR

BOKALI KALESI

8

A

2

3

B

C

1

D

Dardanelles

RUSSELL'S TOP

Main Turkish frontline
opposing 'Anzac' (three
divisions)

Boundary of 'Anzac' (three
divisions plus detachments)

A *Rhododendron Ridge*
B *Quinn's Post*
C *Courtney's Post*
D *Brighton Beach*

Tepe also ground to a halt, and the troops began to dig in. As did Stopford: Hamilton encountered him supervising the construction of dug-outs instead of conducting the battle being fought by his corps. An attempt by 53rd Division to take Scimitar Hill (between the Salt Lake and the Anafarta ridge) on the following day also failed.

Stalemate Again

At this stage of the battle, it should have been obvious that the operation had not succeeded. The 'Anzac breakout' had achieved little, and although the Suvla beachhead was secure, the hills around were still held by the Turks, penning in the British. As the war correspondent Ellis Ashmead-Bartlett noted, the British had simply landed anew and dug another graveyard. Eighteen thousand casualties had been sustained for little gain, yet despite this and despite Stopford's inaction and his mistrust of the 53rd and newly arrived 54th Divisions as untrained amateurs, further offensives were launched at Suvla.

In the first of these, on 12 August, occurred one of the minor mysteries of the campaign. In an advance intended to precede a full divisional attack on the following day, 163 Brigade (54th Division) advanced towards Kujuk Anafarta. In this operation the 1/5th Norfolk Regiment disappeared; as Hamilton wrote in his dispatch, it was a 'very mysterious thing', for 'not one of them ever came back'. Inquiries after the war failed to solve the problem, and the disappearance of part (not all) of this battalion has even been 'explained' by theories of extra-terrestrial activity and alien spacecraft. Almost certainly in excess of 100 bodies were eventually found in a mass grave, but the fact that the Turks denied all knowledge of the unit and that a rumour suggested that all had been shot through the head serves only to create further speculation. The idea that the remains found by the Graves Registration Unit may represent an atrocity which the Turks wished to conceal is more feasible than ludicrous stories of mysterious clouds and Unidentified Flying Objects, but is founded on not much firmer evidence. However, it does serve to illustrate the confused nature of the fighting on the Gallipoli peninsula, amid terrain so

▲ A link with the heyday of the old Victorian army was Colonel John R. Harvey, who in the previous century had been a genuine example of that rarest of creatures, a 'gentleman ranker'. In a letter of condolence following Harvey's death, a comrade wrote: 'No soldier who had the privilege of serving under him could ever forget his powerful and patriotic inspiration; perhaps one of his finest efforts was his arrival at Anzac when few who were present will ever forget the reception which he had from the remnants of the 4th Norfolks.'

ORDER OF BATTLE
Reinforcements after Suvla
(principal units only)

2nd Mounted Division
1 (1 South Midland) Brigade: Warwickshire Yeomanry; Royal Gloucestershire Hussars; Worcestershire Yeomanry
2 (2 South Midland) Brigade: Royal Buckinghamshire Hussars; Dorsetshire Yeomanry; Berkshire Yeomanry
3 (Notts & Derby) Brigade: Sherwood Rangers; South Notts Hussars; Derbyshire Yeomanry
4 (London) Brigade: 1/ and 3/County of London Yeomanry; 1/City of London Yeomanry
5 Brigade: Hertfordshire Yeomanry; 2/County of London Yeomanry
(2nd Mounted Division re-organized and reinforced in September 1915):
1 Mounted Brigade: 1st South Midland Regiment (previously 1 Brigade); 2nd South Midland Regiment (previously 2 Brigade); 5th Yeomanry Regiment (previously 5 Brigade)
2 Mounted Brigade: 3rd Notts & Derby Regiment (previously 3 Brigade); 4th London Regiment (previously 4 Brigade)
1 Scottish Horse Mounted Brigade: 1/, 2/1, 3/1 Scottish Horse
1 Highland Mounted Brigade: Fife & Forfar Yeomanry, 1/ and 2/Lovat's Scouts

2nd Australian Division
5 Australian Brigade: 17th–20th New South Wales Battalions
6 Australian Brigade: 21st–24th Victoria Battalions
7 Australian Brigade: 25th Queensland, 26th Queensland and Tasmania, 27th S. Australia, 28th W. Australia Battalions
Divisional Troops: 13th Victoria Light Horse

South-Eastern Mounted Brigade:
Royal East Kent Yeomanry; West Kent Yeomanry; Sussex Yeomanry

2 South-Western Mounted Brigade:
West Somerset Yeomanry; Royal 1st Devon Yeomanry; Royal North Devon Yeomanry

Eastern Mounted Brigade
Welsh Horse; Norfolk Yeomanry; Loyal Suffolk Hussars

Lowland Mounted Brigade:
Ayrshire Yeomanry; Lanarkshire Yeomanry

rough that the exact events of much of the combat can never be ascertained.

An unsuccessful attempt on Kiritch Tepe was made by 10th Division on 15 August, but before a further operation was mounted, changes in command at last took place. Hamilton very belatedly contacted Kitchener and suggested that Stopford be relieved; Kitchener replied that three good generals (Byng, Maude and Fanshawe) were being sent from the Western Front, so Hamilton dismissed Stopford and replaced him with Major-General de Lisle, previously commander of the 29th Division at Helles. De Lisle was a tough fighter if not possessed of great vision, but his assumption of command of IX Corps caused Hamilton further problems. Lieutenant-General Sir Bryan Mahon of 10th Division was senior to de Lisle and refused to serve under his command, abandoning his division in the midst of the fighting. Major-General F. Hammersley of 11th Division also left, on 23 August, in a state of collapse. Yet not even the overdue replacement of incompetent generals could rescue the situation

▶ *A cartoon by David Barker which epitomizes the indomitable spirit of the ANZACs: 'Are you wounded, mate?'; 'D'yer think I'm doing this fer fun?'. Note the 'SB' ('stretcher-bearer') brassard.*

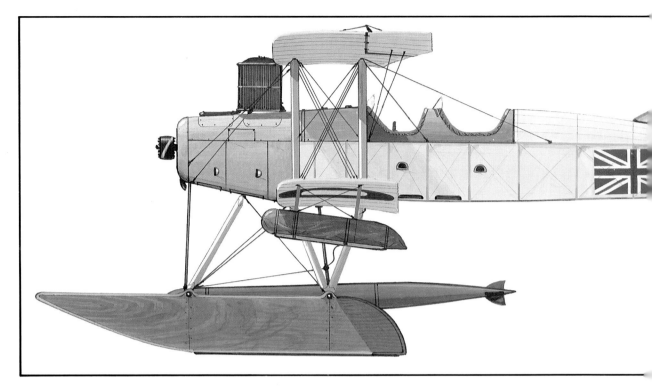

which, thanks to mismanagement and procrastination, was beyond redemption.

Nevertheless, Hamilton resolved upon another assault at Suvla, for which he transferred the veteran 29th Division from Helles. This formation was justly famous, but was no longer the force it had been, worn down as it was by casualties and illness. It was supported by the newly arrived 2nd Mounted Division from Egypt, composed of yeomanry regiments serving as infantry. It was the last real battle of the campaign.

The attack was scheduled for 21 August, in the presence of Hamilton but with de Lisle in actual command. The main attack was to be made upon the Anafarta Spur, at the right by 32 and 34 Brigades (11th Division) upon W Hill, and at the left by 29th Division: 86 Brigade on the left of W Hill and 87 Brigade upon Scimitar Hill. The 53rd and 54th Divisions were to hold the front to the

◀ An Australian rests in a hollow scooped out of the earth, while Captain Phil Fry of the 10th Light Horse poses in the foreground. He wears a typical campaign uniform, including shirt with the lower sleeves cut off and cap with neck-cloth attached. Fry was killed on 29 August in a charge at Hill 60. (Australian War Memorial, neg. no. A 5401)

◄ *Short 184. Original Admiralty Type 184, S106, with ailerons on upper wing only, depicted when shipped aboard the seaplane carrier HMS Benmy-Chree (a converted Isle of Man ferry) in 1915. On 15 August, flown by Flight-Lieutenant Dacre, 184 took part in a torpedo sortie over the Gulf of Saros and successfully attacked a Turkish tug sheltering in False Bay. Along with Short 842, which sank another Turkish ship that day, No. 184 deserves its place in history for the operations in which both aeroplanes were involved were the only air-launched torpedo attacks to be successfully concluded during the First World War. (Painting by Ray Rimell.)*

▼ *A famous name in the Royal Navy: Ark Royal, an ex-merchant ship purchased in May 1914 for use as a seaplane carrier. The aircraft were used primarily for reconnaissance.*

left of 29th Division, and 2nd Mounted Division was to act as reserve. A supporting attack was to be made from Anzac upon Hill 60 by 29 Indian Brigade, elements of 10th and 13th Divisions, and New Zealand Mounted Rifles. The Turks had entrenched before the Anafarta Spur, and thus a heavy bombardment was required, but the artillery assembled was insufficient (32 field-guns, eight 60pdrs, eight 5in howitzers, eight mountain guns and naval gunfire including that of the battleships *Swiftsure* and *Vengeance*). Heavy mist obscured the position to be stormed, rendering artillery direction difficult; Hamilton considered postponing the advance but eventually let it proceed.

Predictably, it was unsuccessful. The 11th Division was unable to attain its objectives, partly because some of its units lost their way, and thus could not support 29th Division's advance on Scimitar Hill. Elements did reach this objective, but were shelled off again. Meanwhile, 2nd Mounted Division advanced across the open plain in support, suffering heavily from artillery fire in the process. The whole force fell back with heavy losses (5,300 from 14,300), but no gain whatever. Only at Anzac was the operation successful, where sufficient ground was taken for the left on Anzac to be joined to the right of Suvla shortly after, forming one continuous front.

EVACUATION

The final main action of the campaign was fought on 29 August, when to secure the junction between Anzac and Suvla, Hill 60 was taken by elements of 29 and 40, 29 Indian and 4 Australian Brigades and two New Zealand Mounted Rifle regiments. They provided a more secure beachhead, but, as at Helles, one which was still overlooked by the Turks. Reinforcements continued to arrive, most notably 5 and 6 Brigades of 2nd Australian Division at Anzac from 20 August, but both sides were fought to a standstill and ravaged by the losses of combat and disease. Only sniping and minor raids continued. The Turks, whose losses had been enormous, now had about half their entire army on the peninsula.

Change of Command

Hamilton reported that he required massive reinforcements for any further progress, and briefly it appeared as if these might be provided by a French proposal to send four new divisions; but this was cancelled when, emboldened by Allied reverses in the Dardanelles, Bulgaria declared war on Serbia. Immediately help had to be sent to Serbia, so instead of receiving more troops, Hamilton lost two divisions, one French and the 10th. In London, an argument was raging over the continued viability of the expedition. Agitation about the mishandling of the campaign was rife in the press; the Australian war correspondent Keith Murdoch wrote a condemnatory letter to the Australian Prime Minister, which report was seen and circulated by Asquith to the members of the Dardanelles Committee. When this was coupled with the dispatches of the English journalist Ellis Ashmead-Bartlett, pressure on the Dardanelles Committee was irresistible. On 11 October Kitchener cabled Hamilton for an assessment of the losses which might be incurred in an evacuation. Unwilling to concede defeat, Hamilton sent a gloomy prognosis that half the men might be lost, but as so many of the troops were raw he thought that an evacuation might be even more catastrophic. This, and the growing disillusionment

◄ *General Sir Charles Monro, who replaced Hamilton in command of the Mediterranean Expeditionary Force after the failure of Suvla.*

▲ *Kitchener (left) and Birdwood (on Kitchener's right) look over a parapet of torn sandbags during Kitchener's visit to the front in November 1915,* *the personal inspection that convinced him of the hopelessness of pursuing the campaign further. (Australian War Memorial, neg. no. G 573)*

over the conduct of the campaign, had a predictable result: Hamilton was relieved of his command and replaced by General Sir Charles Monro, Third Army commander on the Western Front, who was instructed to report on the feasibility of maintaining the effort. In the interim, Birdwood took command of the expedition.

Monro believed that the only sensible strategy was to concentrate resources on the Western Front. He was probably convinced of the hopelessness of the Dardanelles venture even before he visited Helles, Anzac and Suvla in a single day. He found Birdwood anxious to stay, but the other corps commanders (Godley and Byng) in favour of evacuation; and that although the troops at Anzac at least were in good spirits, ammunition was almost exhausted and the expedition ravaged by attritional losses and illness. Monro thus recommended evacuation, which he estimated would cost about 40,000 casualties.

This reply was received with consternation, and Kitchener was sent in person to the Dardanelles, to give a second opinion and (as Asquith admitted) to get him out of the way. At this moment, under the urging of Roger Keyes, the prospect of a renewed naval offensive was raised and even received some support from Kitchener; but although Keyes had supporters, his scheme came to nothing. Monro's determination that the campaign was beyond redemption won over Kitchener, who concluded reluctantly (from personal inspection) that the Gallipoli peninsula was 'an awful place' and that further efforts were useless. Kitchener recommended that Anzac and Suvla be evacuated immediately, that Helles be maintained for a time, and that although Monro should take command of the forces at Salonika, he should remain in overall charge of the Gallipoli forces, while Birdwood (whom Kitchener had wanted to appoint to supreme command) supervised the evacuation.

At this time, two important personalities disappeared from the scene. On 15 November Winston Churchill resigned his government post (Chancellor of the Duchy of Lancaster) and began a period of political eclipse, receiving some of the blame for the failure of the expedition. In early December, after months of leading the main Turkish defence, during which he had been very frequently exposed to intense personal danger, Mustafa Kemal's health broke down under a combination of physical and mental exhaustion, and he left the scene of his triumph.

On the Gallipoli peninsula, both Allies and Turks dug deeper and prepared for winter; none imagined that the British government was about to terminate the campaign, and such was the damage it was causing the Turks that Enver made unofficial approaches to President Wilson of the USA to use his influence to negotiate an end to the war.

Illness on the peninsula decreased with the onset of cooler weather, but the hazards of a Gallipoli winter were demonstrated by a blizzard which began on 27 November. After three days 200 men had frozen to death or drowned in the torrents which flooded the dry water-courses and trenches, and at Suvla alone at least 5,000 men were disabled by frostbite. The Turks suffered equally.

The Withdrawal

In contrast to the remainder of the campaign, the evacuation was a triumph of organization and discipline; that it was uncontested was attributable to the Allied plan of deception. The troops at Anzac and Suvla were informed on 12 December that they were to be taken off, but to conceal this from the Turks empty supply-boxes were taken in during the day, and at night men were taken off from the jetties which had been built on the beaches. To complete the illusion, as the numbers of troops dwindled, the full complement of cooking-fires continued to be lit, and the artillery continued to fire their previous daily quota of shells. By the morning of 18 December half the force had been withdrawn (40,000 men), with most of their equipment; 20,000 more got away on the night of the 18th, leaving a precarious bridgehead of only 20,000. This final evacuation was that most fraught with danger, should the Allies' exodus be discovered. At this time the Suvla/Anzac front was held by the following units, running north to south: at the left flank of Suvla, 11th Division; 88 Brigade (29th Division) north of

◀ *Although there was no scope for the employment of cavalry at Gallipoli, horses were used as draught animals and, together with motor-cycles, as the transport for couriers. This dispatch-rider gallops at full speed past a cemetery at Anzac.*

The Evacuation, 8/9 June 1915

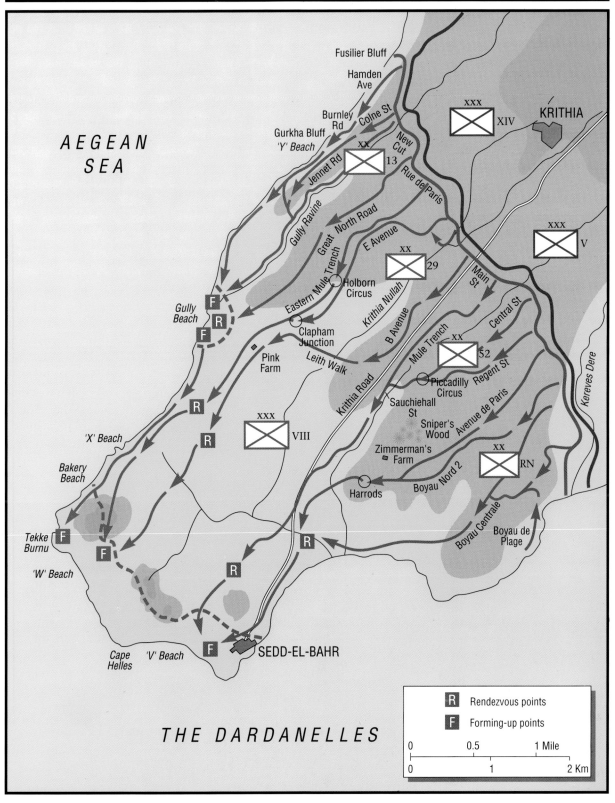

AEGEAN SEA

Fusilier Bluff

Hamden Ave

Burnley Rd

Colne St

Gurkha Bluff

'Y' Beach

New Cut

KRITHIA

XXX — XIV

XX — 13

Jennet Rd

Rue de Paris

Gully Ravine

Great North Road

E Avenue

XXX — V

Main St

XX — 29

Eastern Mule Trench

Holborn Circus

Krithia Nullah

B Avenue

Central St

Gully Beach

F
R
F

Clapham Junction

Leith Walk

Pink Farm

Krithia Road

Mule Trench

XX — 52

Regent St

Piccadilly Circus

Sauchiehall St

Avenue de Paris

'X' Beach

R

R

XXX — VIII

Sniper's Wood

Zimmerman's Farm

XX — RN

Bakery Beach

Harrods

Boyau Nord 2

Kereves Dere

Tekke Burnu

F
F

R

R

Boyau Centrale

Boyau de Plage

'W' Beach

Cape Helles

'V' Beach

F

SEDD-EL-BAHR

THE DARDANELLES

| | R | Rendezvous points |
| | F | Forming-up points |

0   0.5   1 Mile

0   1   2 Km

the Salt Lake; 13th Division; 2nd Mounted Division at the right flank of Suvla. (The 53rd Division, the remaining two brigades of 29th Division, and 34 Brigade of 11th Division had been withdrawn earlier.) At the junction of the Suvla/Anzac boundary, 29 Indian Brigade; Australian and New Zealand Division; 2nd Australian Division; 1st Australian Division; and at the right flank of Anzac, 2 Light Horse Brigade. To the left of the 29th Indians was a newly arrived yeomanry formation of the Welsh Horse, Norfolk and Suffolk Yeomanry, which had been attached to 54th Division.

So that the Turks would not realize that the front line would eventually be deserted, automatically firing rifles were devised by the use of water-powered weights or candles which burned through strings to pull the triggers of fixed rifles, so that for half an hour after the troops had left, occasional shots would be directed towards the Turkish lines; and a mine was dug under Chunuk Bair. On the night of the 19th the entire force fell back by degrees, along pre-arranged routes to designated forming-up and beachhead defensive positions. By dawn on 20 December every man had been taken off, for the loss of two men wounded at Anzac and not a casualty at Suvla. Only when the mine exploded at Chunuk Bair did the Turks realize that something had happened, but by the time they progressed to the beaches through wire entanglements and booby traps to appropriate those supplies which could not be taken off, the entire Allied force had gone.

Liman von Sanders immediately began to organize the best of his tired divisions for an assault on Helles; in all he could muster 21 divisions to oppose just four Allied divisions. The Helles position was obviously untenable, and Monro's advice was accepted: Helles must be evacuated. Monro himself was posted to command First Army on the Western Front, and the

▼*Packed like sardines, stretcher-cases and 'walking wounded' are evacuated from Anzac by tugboats and barges;* *photographed by Chaplain E. N. Merrington. (Australian War Memorial, neg. no. C 2679)*

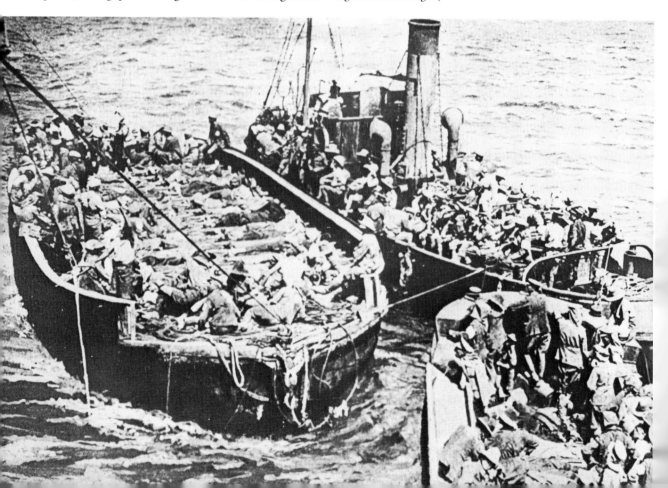

responsiblity for the last stage was entrusted to Birdwood, de Robeck, and Keyes. In order to facilitate transmission of orders in a potentially hazardous operation, the remaining French were withdrawn immediately, less their artillery, which was on loan to the British until the end. To fill the gap, the battered 29th Division was pushed back into the line and 13th Division, now experienced in evacuation in the face of the enemy, replaced 42nd Division. The 11th Division was retained temporarily in the Aegean for use as a reserve, and the remaining troops from Anzac and Suvla were sent to Egypt to recuperate. At Helles, the defences were manned from left to right by: 13th Division; 29th Division; 52nd Division; and, in the old French sector, the Royal Naval Division.

Again it was a phased withdrawal, so that by 7 January, of the approximate 40,000 men and 150

▼ *The funeral pyre of the Gallipoli expedition: burning stores photographed from the sea after the final evacu-* ation. *Note the naval gun-barrel at the left. (Australian War Memorial, neg. no. A 3312)*

guns at Helles at the end of December, only 19,000 were left. At this moment, Liman von Sanders launched his last attack. It should have fallen two days earlier, but Enver Pasha had interfered again and ordered the withdrawal of nine divisions. Under Liman von Sanders' threat of resignation he countermanded the order, but it delayed the great attack. This came under the cover of the heaviest bombardment of the campaign, directed principally upon the British left flank, and mounted by the Turkish XIV Corps (V Corps held the line opposite the British right; Turkish divisional sectors from the British left to right were held by the 12th, 10th, 13th and 14th Divisions). The attack failed almost before it had begun: it was met by steady British fire, and many Turks simply refused to advance, as if, after months of heroism, their will had finally given out. This last and potentially most devastating attack cost the British just 164 casualties, almost all among the 7th North Staffordshire Regiment of 39 Brigade (13th Division), whose trenches were heavily shelled.

On the night of 8/9 January 1916 a repeat of the last evacuation of Suvla and Anzac was arranged at Helles: a withdrawal along arranged routes, in complete silence, with automatically firing rifles; 'V' and 'W' Beaches were the main embarkation points. Shortly before 4 a.m. on 9 January the abandoned ammunition-dumps blew up, to be answered by a Turkish bombardment; but not a man was left ashore, and not a casualty had been sustained. The evacuation of Gallipoli was a triumph, closing a campaign of incompetence.

Assessment:

Despite the enormous damage it caused to the Turkish Army and national resources, the Gallipoli campaign was undoubtedly a disaster for the Allies, who had sent some half a million men to the Dardanelles, of whom about half became casualties; Turkish losses were slightly more, just over a quarter of a million. Probably about 87,000 Turks, 25,000 British, almost 10,000 French, 7,300 Australians, 2,400 New Zealanders and

▲ *The Turkish War Medal, often (but erroneously) described as 'the Gallipoli Star' from its institution at the beginning of the campaign* *(1 March). A white-metal star with red enamel decoration, it was awarded for distinguished service and worn without a ribbon on the left breast.*

1,700 Indians lost their lives in what was, in the final reckoning, a futile campaign. Gallipoli wrecked many reputations, especially that of Kitchener, whose drowning in HMS *Hampshire* saved him from the ultimate decline of his influence; and Hamilton, who never again commanded in the field. Liman von Sanders continued to command Turkish forces until he was defeated by Allenby in 1918; Enver Pasha went into exile following the collapse of 1918 and apparently died in action in Turkestan in 1922. Winston Churchill recovered his reputation and returned to government in 1917. Mustafa Kemal, the energetic driving-force behind the gallant Turkish defence of the peninsula, rose to supreme power as Kemal Ataturk, 'Father of the Turks', becoming that nation's outstanding personality of the modern era. If the Gallipoli experience was a major factor in the emergence of new Turkish nationhood, so it was for Australia and New Zealand, forging a sense of national identity and establishing a reputation which endures. The day of the landings, 25 April, is celebrated as ANZAC Day, Australia's proudest anniversary. Locations like Anzac Cove, Lone Pine and Lancashire Landing have passed into folklore. Above all, the impression of Gallipoli is one of a valid strategic concept ruined by catastrophic incompetence, over which not even the heroism displayed at every turn could emerge victorious.

The sense of futility affected all those who emerged alive from Gallipoli. In a letter of condolence to the father of Edmund Priestman of the 6th Battalion, The York and Lancaster Regiment, who fell at Suvla, a fellow-officer remarked that 'Few of us were spared. The bravest and best were taken.' Equally true and equally poignant was the verse *Anzac* by 'Argent', published in *Passing Show* and reprinted in the memoir of 'Trooper Bluegum' (Oliver Hogue) in 1916:

> 'And all of our trouble wasted!
>   all of it gone for nix!
> Still . . . we kept our end up –
>   and some of the story sticks.
> Fifty years on in Sydney
>   they'll talk of our first big fight,
> And even in little old, blind old England,
>   possibly some one might.'

THE BATTLEFIELD TODAY

When Alan Moorhead wrote his famous *Gallipoli* in 1956, he noted that apart from the occasional organized tour, the battlefield was visited by scarcely half a dozen people per year. Tours are more frequent now, but unlike many battlefields which have disappeared beneath modern development, the area is virtually as deserted now as it was in 1915. The tip of the peninsula is a Turkish national park, which has prevented building and the more obtrusive type of tourist attraction, though forestation has altered the appearance of parts of the scene of the tragedy of 1915.

The Turks are commemorated by some monuments, but on the entire battlefield there is only one Turkish war grave, of a heroic sergeant killed at Sari Bair, which has to represent the rest: during the campaign the Turks made no effort to bury their dead, simply shovelling them into ravines or pits, and no attempt was made after the war to recover the remains. In sharp contrast are the 31 Commonwealth cemeteries within 25 miles of Cape Helles, but as no Army Graves Unit was able to visit the area until after the war most of the original markers had been lost, so that unidentified burials form a greater proportion than in other war cemeteries. The cemeteries are grouped in three main areas: Helles, Anzac and Suvla; the dead were mostly allowed to lie where they fell, instead of being collected into larger burial-grounds. They vary in size as a result, from almost 3,000 graves at Greenhill Cemetery, Suvla, to less than 100 at Walker's Ridge Cemetery, Anzac; and memorials stand at Helles, overlooking the landing-beaches where so many died, commemorating almost 21,000; at Lone Pine (almost 5,000); and at Chunuk Bair (852). The cemeteries often bear the names given to the locations at the time of the campaign and add a dreadful poignancy to the resting-place of thousands: Baby 700, Embarkation Pier, Lone Pine, Quinn's Post, Shell Green,

▲*Rhododendron Ridge.
(Australian War Memorial,
neg. no. G 1810 B)*

Shrapnel Valley, all at Anzac; Lala Baba Cemetery at Suvla, which includes the grave of Brigadier-General Paul Kenna, who died on 30 August, and who had won the Victoria Cross with the 21st Lancers at Omdurman; and at Helles, Lancashire Landing (where lies William Keneally, one of the 1st Lancashire Fusiliers' 'six VCs before breakfast'), Pink Farm, Redoubt, Skew Bridge, Twelve Tree Copse (where lies the last Gallipoli VC, Second-Lieutenant Alfred Smith of the 1/5th East Lancashires, who threw himself upon a grenade to save his men from the blast); and 'V' Beach Cemetery, containing the graves of Lieutenant-Colonel Charles Doughty-Wylie (staff), and Captain Garth Walford of the Royal Artillery, both VCs killed on 26 April. Such memorials are almost the only signs that a terrible and bitter campaign was fought in this area; and it is surely to be regretted that almost none of the brave Turkish defenders lie in marked graves.

CHRONOLOGY

31 October 1914: declaration of war on Turkey by Britain, France and Russia.

19 February 1915: Admiral Carden's first bombardment of Dardanelles defences.

25 February 1915: Carden's second bombardment.

12 March: Ian Hamilton appointed to command Mediterranean Expeditionary Force.

13 March: abortive attempt to sweep mines from Dardanelles channel.

18 March: Admiral de Robeck's great naval attack.

26 March: Otto Liman von Sanders takes command of Turkish forces at Gallipoli.

25 April: landings at Helles and Anzac.

26 April: consolidation at Helles and Anzac; evacuation of 'Y' Beach.

28 April: First Battle of Krithia.

1 May: Turkish attack at Helles.

6–8 May: Second Battle of Krithia.

12 May: sinking of HMS *Goliath* causes abandonment of second naval attack.

19–20 May: Turkish attacks at Anzac.

24 May: truce at Anzac to bury dead.

25 May: submarine operations: Nasmith in *E 11* sinks freighter at Constantinople, Hersing in *U 21* sinks *Triumph*.

26 May: Asquith announces coalition government.

4 June: Third Battle of Krithia.

21 June: French capture of trenches at right of Helles.

28 June: Allied line pushed to Fusilier Bluff.

28 June: ANZAC diversionary attack.

28/29 June: Turkish attack on Quinn's Post–Pope's Hill sector of Anzac.

30 June: Gouraud wounded.

12/13 July: British offensive at Helles.

4–6 August: secret reinforcement to Anzac.

6 August: diversionary attack at Helles.

6 August: British landing at Suvla.

6–9 August: ANZAC attack at Lone Pine; attempted 'Anzac breakout'.

7 August: charge of 3 Light Horse Brigade, Russell's Top.

9 August: British attack at Suvla.

12 August: British attack at Suvla.

12/13 August: Turkish counter-attack at Helles.

15 August: British attack at Kiritch Tepe.

21 August: major British attack at Suvla.

29 August: capture of Hill 60.

16 October: Hamilton replaced in command.

28 October: Monro takes command of expedition.

22 November: Kitchener recommends evacuation.

27–30 November: great storm at Gallipoli.

8 December: Monro ordered to evacuate Suvla and Anzac.

12 December: troops at Suvla and Anzac told of plan to evacuate.

19–20 December: evacuation of Suvla and Anzac.

7 January 1916: last Turkish attack at Helles.

8–9 January 1916: final evacuation of Helles, with end of campaign.

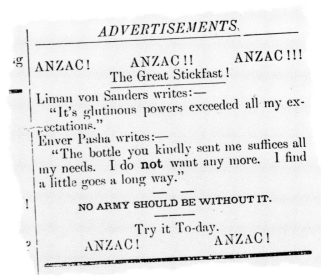

A GUIDE TO FURTHER READING

Among the many works on Gallipoli, the British Official History (*Military Operations, Gallipoli*, Brigadier-General C. F. Aspinall-Oglander, London, 1929–32) is among the most important, though inevitably reserved in its criticism; C. E. W. Bean's *Official History of Australia in the War of 1914–18* (Sydney, 1921–43) contains much of value. Alan Moorhead's *Gallipoli* (London, 1956) is deservedly regarded as a literary classic; the latest edition (London, 1989) is expanded and with added illustrations. John Laffin's *Damn the Dardanelles* (London, 1980) is a critical study which points the finger of blame; *Gallipoli: One Long Grave* (Kit Denton, Sydney, 1986) is especially well-illustrated, as is *Images of Gallipoli* (P. A. Pedersen, Melbourne and Oxford, 1988). Robert Rhodes James's *Gallipoli* (London, 1965) is a good modern account; Major-General C. E. Callwell's *The Dardanelles* (London, 1919) contains interesting comments on the strategic and tactical aspects; *The Suvla Bay Landing* (J. Hargrave, London, 1964) incorporates the author's personal experiences of that phase of the campaign. *The French and the Dardanelles* (G. H. Cassar, London, 1971) is useful for the French view, and Hans Kannengiesser's *The Campaign of Gallipoli* (London, 1927) is a convenient source for the Turkish/German view. Ian Hamilton's *Gallipoli Diary* (London, 1920) and *Despatches from the Dardanelles, etc.* (London, 1917) are significant; Norman Wilkinson's *The Dardanelles, etc.* (London, 1915) reproduces many of his magnificent watercolours. Personal accounts are legion: Peter Liddle's *Men of Gallipoli* (London, 1976) – which has an extensive bibliography – and *Gallipoli 1915: Pens, Pencils and Cameras at War* (London, 1985) make extensive use of first-hand accounts, and among useful contemporary works are *With the 29th Division in Gallipoli* (Revd. O. Creighton, London, 1916), *With a B-P Scout in Gallipoli* (E. Y. Priestman, London, 1916) (which describes the training of a New Army battalion), and *Trooper Bluegum at the Dardanelles* (O. Hogue, London, 1916). *The Anzac Book* (London, 1916) is a celebration of the spirit of the Australian and New Zealand fighting men.

ODE TO TENEDOS.

O Tenedos, thy peaceful island green
A stirring passage in the fight has seen;
Eight generals and half-a-hundred men
First packed their kit, and then unpacked again.

CORRESPONDENCE.

Sir,—As a strict grammarian my ear is offended by the prevalent system of referring to officers, recalled for service during the war, as "Dug Outs." May I suggest that this form of the plural is strictly ungrammatical, and that the name should be spelt "Dugs Out."

Yours etc.,
PETER PAN.

Where the Helles the Harem.

TO LET.

Several excellent houses in Sedd-el-Bahr, specially recommended for those undergoing open air treatment.

Illustrating the characteristic of 'humour in adversity', snippets from the 'newspaper'

Dardanelles Driveller which reduced to a joke the most arduous aspects of the campaign.

WARGAMING GALLIPOLI

Despite the existence of several excellent ranges of wargames figures, complemented by sets of rules ranging from the highly complex to the simple, the First World War has never attracted a wide following among wargamers. One reason may well be the apparent problem of gaming large set-piece battles of the type that seemed to predominate on the Western Front. As map games or large-scale table-top games they seem to have little to offer because, with few exceptions, little ground was gained and commanders tended to lose control of the action once the troops were out of their trenches. Large- and small-scale trench raid games, often played with 20mm or 15mm scale figures, can be very interesting but tend to be somewhat repetitive if played frequently. On the naval side the desire to bring about decisive fleet actions – an obsession seemingly shared by wargamers and the admirals commanding the British and German fleets – has tended to blind many wargamers to the wider possibilities offered by the period. It is only the development of aerial warfare during the Great War that seems to have really attracted any noticeable following amongst wargamers; but even here there has been a tendency to concentrate on fighter combat rather than all aspects of early aerial warfare.

The Gallipoli Campaign, as this book shows, provides an excellent background for wargamers who want to get to grips with gaming the First World War. The scale and scope of the campaign offers wargamers the possibility of experiencing a wide range of different games within a manageable framework. A battalion attack on the Western Front, for example, would have been a tiresome pin-prick; on Gallipoli it could have been decisive.

The Allied attempts to capture Constantinople, of which the Gallipoli Campaign forms a part, can be split into several inter-connecting phases, each of which can be wargamed in a different way. These phases are:

1. The Allied attempt to force the Narrows.
2. The exploits of the Allied submarines in the Dardanelles and the Bosporous.
3. The landings at Cape Helles and Anzac Cove.
4. The Allied attempts to break-out of their bridge-heads.
5. The landings at Suvla Bay.
6. The Evacuation.

Forcing the Narrows

Until recently any wargamers wishing to game the Allied naval bombardment of the Turkish forts guarding the entrance to the Dardanelles would have had to draw up their own rules for ship-to-shore gunfire. As radio-equipped airborne spotters were not available to the attacking warships, such gunfire would have been somewhat more 'hit-and-miss' than the standard achieved later in the War. This can be simulated by forcing the Allied players to 'guesstimate' the range, which would then be measured and adjusted up or down, left or right, by the umpire. The umpire would 'generate' the degree of error by throwing two normal dice, adding their scores together, and reading the result from the following table:

Dice Score	Degree of Error
2, 7, 12	No adjustment
3, 4	Down 100 yards
5	Down 200 yards
10, 11	Up 100 yards
9	Up 200 yards
6	Right 100 yards
8	Left 100 yards

These results are for naval guns firing at ranges between 1,000 and 2,500 yards; for ranges between 2,500 yards and 5,000 yards double the error; for ranges beyond 5,000 yards treble the error; for ranges below 1,000 yards halve the error.' The Turkish players would not need to 'guesstimate' the ranges for their shore batteries; they would measure the range to their target as per normal. An alternative system to that outlined above is now available in the form of a reprint of Fred T. Jane's 1912 edition of *How to Play the 'Naval Wargame'*. Jane's rules contain a specific section that deals with ship-to-shore and shore-to-ship gunfire. Since these rules were used as a teaching aid by some Royal Navy officers of the period, it seems appropriate to use them here.

B11 and E11

Both before and during the Gallipoli campaign, Allied submarines succeeded in breaking into the Dardanelles and, during the latter part of the campaign, the Bosporous. As a result, the Turks lost two predreadnought battleships sunk – the *Messudieh* by the British submarine *B11* and the *Hairredin Barbarossa* by the British submarine *E11* – and seaborne reinforcements and supplies to the Turkish troops fighting the Allies were disrupted. An excellent game that re-created the exploits of the *B11* and her compatriots was published in *Wargames World 2* in 1988 and is still available from Wargame Developments. With a little re-working, the basic structure could be expanded to encompass the later break-through into the Bosporous by *E11*. The game has many similarities to a fantasy-style game in that the submarine commander gives his orders to the umpire (or games-master), who then tells them what is or is not going on around their submarine. It is a challenging game with one or two nasty twists in it!

The Landings at Cape Helles and Anzac Cove

The pre-landing preparations by both the Allies and the Turks can best be simulated by using the Committee Game format popularized by members of Wargame Developments. On the Turkish side the various players (including the German 'advisers') should be given different goals to achieve: e.g., Kemal needs to prevent a total take-over by the Germans, while ensuring that their help is

retained; von Sanders needs to keep the Turks in alliance with the Central Powers but also needs the defences of the approaches to Constantinople to be effective (i.e., under German control). The British players would have different problems to solve: e.g., co-operation between the Army and the Navy, between the British and the French, and between the British and the 'Colonials'.

The landings themselves can be played out as either a map game or as a table-top game. Certainly the approach by sea to the landing sites can best be gamed on the map, and the navigational errors suffered can be simulated by giving each player a slightly different version of the map from that used by the umpire. Once the Allied forces reach the drop-off point for the ships' boats used to land the troops, the action can be transferred to the table-top. The terrain can be re-created by putting the beach at one end of the table and building up a high plateau at the other end. Access to the top of the plateau would only be available by narrow gullies in the slope leading up to the plateau. The whole gully and plateau area can then be liberally sprinkled with lichen and cat litter or fine gravel to simulate the rocky, scrub-covered terrain found on the Gallipoli Peninsula.

An alternative method could be the use of terrain cards. This was first described in Peter Gritton's article on 'Wargaming Night Actions', which was published in the first issue of *Wargames Illustrated*. A grid of playing cards is laid out, face down, on the table-top. As the assaulting troops reach the grid the card in front of them is turned over. This 'generates' the terrain to their front: e.g., Ace of Spades = unclimbable gully; 6 of Hearts = climbable gully covered by a Turkish machine-gun; 7 of Clubs = sheer rock face. This system re-creates the uncertainty of landing on the wrong beach for which the commander has an inappropriate and inaccurate map. The Turkish forces are best left under the control of the umpire as, to a certain extent, the disposition of their forces will be determined by the terrain cards.

The use of ships' boats to transport the assault troops to the beach while under fire from the shore does not often occur in a wargame. As the troops in the boats are more likely to survive the sinking of their boat the closer they are to the shore, the following method can be used to calculate a percentage survival rate:

$$100 - \frac{Range\ in\ Yards}{50} \times \frac{Range\ in\ Yards}{50} = \text{Percentage chance of troops reaching the shore safely}$$

(E.g.: A ship's boat is hit and sunk 400 yards from the shore; the troops in the boat have a 36 per cent chance of reaching the shore safely. A ship's boat is hit and sunk 200 yards from the shore; the troops in the boat have an 84 per cent chance of reaching the shore safely.)

The Allies Try to Break-Out

Once the respective front-lines had stabilized, the style of warfare became similar to that on the Western Front and can be re-created on the table-top in the same way. It is important to remember, however, that had either the Turks or the Allies managed a decisive break-through, even with quite a small force, the campaign *could* have come to a rapid conclusion. This should make a battalion or brigade-sized trench attack somewhat more appealing to play through. For the wargamer interested in small-scale skirmish games, certain specific types of operation, while not unique to the Gallipoli campaign, can be made into a good game. These include 'Hunting the Sniper' – both sides employed very skilled snipers and the Turks, in particular, were renowned for their ingenious camouflage – and 'Clearing the Trench'. Examples of both these types of operation were vividly re-created in the Australian television drama series, *ANZACS*.

The Suvla Bay Landings

This is one of the great 'what ifs?' of the campaign. Had the landings succeeded, then the campaign would have probably come to a very rapid conclusion. The landings can be re-created as a map game, or a table-top game, or as a combination of the two. In the latter case an ideal method would be set up a small mega-game; in other words, put the opposing commanders and their staffs in separate rooms, and only allow them to communicate with their front-line commanders via the umpire(s) or by telephone. The umpire(s) could then either play-out the action on a map or table-top – what Wargame Developments call being a 'plumpire' (player/umpire) – or oversee the actions of players who have taken on the roles of front-line commanders. This method never fails to create 'the fog of war' and is a salutary reminder that in real war high-level commanders rarely have anything but tenuous control over their forces.

The Evacuation

Wargamers are very rarely interested in gaming retreats, even successful ones. The evacuation of the Allied troops from Gallipoli rates as one of the outstanding achievements of the Great War and was due almost entirely to excellent planning. It should, therefore, appeal to those wargamers whose interests lie in staff operations and logistics. Such wargamers are few and far between and are often solo players. It is probable, therefore, that the best approach to re-creating this type of operation can probably be found in the pages of *Lone Warrior*, the journal of the Solo Wargamers' Association.

What Ifs?

Although the Gallipoli Campaign did not achieve the goals intended for it, several decisive opportunities could have presented themselves to both sides. Some are summarized here:

1. What would have happened if the Allied fleet had forced the Narrows and reached Constantinople?
2. What would have happened if the Allied fleet had been accompanied by a small landing force of marines?
3. What would have happened if the Turkish fleet had managed to disrupt the landings at Cape Helles and Anzac Cove?
4. What would have happened had either side broken-through the other's front-line?
5. What would have happened if the Turks had not been deceived, and had attacked as the evacuation was being undertaken?

One of the joys of wargaming is asking these questions – and finding the answers!